EASY
CHRISTMAS
CRAFTS

SUSAN COUSINEAU

NORTH LIGHT BOOKS
CINCINNATI, OHIO

www.artistsnetwork.com

about the author

SUSAN COUSINEAU is a freelance designer and author living with her husband, Tom, and their very spoiled pets, in the picturesque town of Fort Frances, Ontario. Christmas has always been Susan's favorite time of year, and her love of this festive season is continually reflected in her design and decorating style. In fact, it was her papier mâché Santa designs that landed her first book contracts back in 1993.

Although this is Susan's first endeavor with North Light Books, she has authored twelve previous booklets and has contributed to ten multidesigner books since the start of her professional design career. Several of Susan's designs have also been published by national craft magazines and have appeared on numerous book and magazine covers. Susan has an honors degree in business administration and recently obtained her diploma in computer graphic design.

Susan hopes this book inspires you to fill your heart and home with the simple pleasures of Christmas as you celebrate the joy and magic of this enchanting holiday season.

07 06 05 04 03   5 4 3 2 1

Library of Congress Cataloging-in-Publication Data
Cousineau, Susan.
Easy Christmas crafts / Susan Cousineau.
  p. cm.
Includes index.
ISBN 1-58180-445-8 (pbk.: alk. paper)
1. Christmas decorations. 2. Handicraft. I. Title.
TT900.C4.C696 2003
745.594'12--dc21

2002043184

Editor: Jolie Lamping Roth
Designer: Andrea Short
Layout Artist: Karla Baker
Production Coordinator: Michelle Ruberg
Photographers: Tim Grondin, Christine Polomsky and Al Parrish
Photo Stylist: Jan Nickum

METRIC CONVERSION CHART

TO CONVERT	TO	MULTIPLY BY
Inches	Centimeters	2.54
Centimeters	Inches	0.4
Feet	Centimeters	30.5
Centimeters	Feet	0.03
Yards	Meters	0.9
Meters	Yards	1.1
Sq. Inches	Sq. Centimeters	6.45
Sq. Centimeters	Sq. Inches	0.16
Sq. Feet	Sq. Meters	0.09
Sq. Meters	Sq. Feet	10.8
Sq. Yards	Sq. Meters	0.8
Sq. Meters	Sq. Yards	1.2
Pounds	Kilograms	0.45
Kilograms	Pounds	2.2
Ounces	Grams	28.4
Grams	Ounces	0.04

Grampa, Auntie Mary, Michael and me —1965

Mom, Dad, Michael and me—Christmas 1965

dedication

My childhood Christmases are full of magical memories. I remember the anticipation of the first snowfall, tobogganing on the riverbank, building snow forts and skating on Biddeson Creek. Each holiday season brought Mom's mouthwatering spritz cookies, the spicy scent of our beautifully flocked Christmas tree, and the long-awaited arrival of the three gallant wisemen perched upon our snowy rooftop.

This book is dedicated to those magical times, and to the family and friends who gave me such a wonderful gift of childhood Christmas memories. I would like to share this gift with you through some of my favorite photos of holidays past.

I hope your Christmas is filled with the merriest of memories as you celebrate the spirit of the season.

acknowledgments

Special thanks to my family for your continued encouragement and support, especially my husband, Tom; Pops and Laurie; Auntie Mary; and Michael and Karen.

I would also like to express my sincere thanks to North Light Books for this wonderful opportunity and to the very talented crew who made this book a reality: Tricia Waddell, for opening this "window of opportunity"; my editor, Jolie Lamping Roth, for all her guidance and hard work; Tim Grondin, for taking such beautiful photos; and Andrea Short, for her creative book design. It has been a pleasure working with all of you.

My heartfelt thanks also goes out to all the companies who so generously provided the supplies for this book: Creative Paperclay Company (Michael Gerbasi), Delta Technical Coatings, Inc. (Barbara Carson), DecoArt, Inc. (Rosemary Reynolds), Loew-Cornell, Inc. (Shirley Miller), FloraCraft/Dow Styrofoam (Sharon Currier), Duncan Enterprises (Linda Bagby), Activa Products, Inc. (Frank Strauss) and Sterling, Inc. (Samantha Hammontree).

Michael and me—Waiting for Santa Christmas 1966

TABLE OF *Contents*

1. VISIONS OF SUGARPLUMS

2. SANTA CLAUS LANE

3. FROSTY FUN

4. TEDDY BEAR TREASURES

5. GLITTERS OF CHRISTMAS PAST

tools & materials

*H*ere's a brief introduction to some of the basic supplies you will need to create the projects in this book. For a complete listing of the supplies required for each project, please refer to the individual project instructions.

★ LOEW-CORNELL BRUSHES

- Series 410: ⅛-inch (3mm), ¼-inch (6mm) and ⅜-inch (10mm) deerfoot stippler brushes.

I use the deerfoot stipplers for drybrushing cheeks. The brush size you choose will depend on the size of the cheek area for each project. You can also use old "fluffy" brushes of various sizes for the dry-brush technique.

The American Painter 4000 Series brushes used to create the projects in this book include:

- Series 4000: nos. 3 and 5 round brushes
- Series 4300: nos. 4, 6 and 8 shader (flat) brushes
- Series 4350: 10/0 or no. 0 liner brush (for painting fine details and delicate lines)
- Series 4550: ¾-inch (2cm) wash brush (great for basecoating large areas)

★ GENERAL PAINTING SUPPLIES

Below are the general painting supplies you will need to create the projects in this book:

- Delta Ceramcoat acrylic paints (refer to individual project instructions for required colors)
- an old, worn toothbrush (for projects that are spattered)
- brush basin or water tub (to rinse brushes)
- paper towels
- palette or wax paper

★ MISCELLANEOUS SUPPLIES

The projects in this book require a number of miscellaneous supplies. Some of the more obvious or readily available supplies, such as a ruler, pencil or scissors, are mentioned here, but they are not mentioned in the projects' materials lists. Skim through each project's instructions before beginning to make sure you have everything within reach.

- ruler, sharp knife and scissors
- glue gun/glue sticks
- tacky glue
- blow-dryer (to speed up the drying process)

(CLOCKWISE FROM TOP RIGHT): Loew-Cornell brushes, Delta Ceramcoat acrylic paints, Delta Ceramcoat interior varnish (brush-on and spray), iridescent crystal glitter, Delta Freshly Fallen Snow, DecoArt Snow-Tex, palette knives, more brushes, and Tulip dimensional paints.

- various Styrofoam shapes
- palette knives (straight or trowel shaped) to apply Snow-Tex
- Tulip (or Scribbles) Dimensional Paints (refer to individual project instructions for required colors)
- compressed sponges
- fine-point black permanent pen (Pigma Micron 05 or Zig Memory System 05)

★ TRANSFERRING PATTERNS

The following are materials you will need to transfer the patterns on pages 55–60. If you do not wish to transfer the patterns, use them as a guide and freehand the details. For directions on transferring patterns and creating templates, see page 54.

- transparent tracing paper
- gray transfer paper
- pencil and eraser (can also use a ballpoint pen to transfer patterns)
- lightweight cardboard or posterboard (if making templates)

★ SNOW TEXTURE MEDIUM

I've found two products that work great for giving the illusion of snow: Snow-Tex and Freshly Fallen Snow.

- DecoArt Snow-Tex creates a snowy dimensional effect on a wide variety of craft surfaces, including Styrofoam shapes, wood, papier mâché, metal and plastic. It's perfect for adding a snowy look to pine wreaths, garlands, miniature trees, pinecones and your favorite Christmas trims.

- Delta Freshly Fallen Snow gives the look of real icing and is great for frosting your Sugarplum Cottage (see page 14). It also gives a wonderful snow-tipped look to your Christmas pine sprays, wreaths, trims and accessories.

★ AIR-DRY MODELING CLAY

Creative Paperclay is a wonderful air-dry clay that is extremely pliable and great for creating projects with a smooth, lightweight finish. It can be molded by itself or applied onto a Styrofoam base. It can also be flattened with a rolling pin, just like cookie dough. Once rolled, you can press your favorite cookie cutter shapes into the flattened clay to make delightful ornaments.

I use Creative Paperclay in all of the projects calling for an air-dry modeling clay, but you can use any brand you feel comfortable working with.

★ INSTANT PAPIER MÂCHÉ

Celluclay Instant Papier Mâché is a great alternative to traditional papier mâché techniques. No strips of newspapers or messy paste are required. You simply mix the prepackaged paper pulp with water in a mixing bowl and you have an "instant" papier mâché mixture to work with. This mixture can be applied onto various Styrofoam shapes such as balls, cones and eggs to make delightful Christmas decorations and ornaments.

★ FINISHING MATERIALS

Listed below are some of my favorite finishing materials:

- Delta Ceramcoat matte interior varnish (brush-on)
- Delta Ceramcoat matte interior spray varnish
- DecoArt Glamour Dust
- iridescent crystal glitter

I generally recommend using the brush-on varnish for projects that are sprinkled with DecoArt Glamour Dust and iridescent crystal glitter as it will provide better adhesion.

The spray varnish works great for most projects, though, and is the way to go if you are the impatient type. Once you try both, you'll find what works best for you.

WINTER BRILLIANCE

For a magical touch, sprinkle your snow texture medium with Glamour Dust and iridescent crystal glitter.

painting terms & techniques

Below is a list of general painting terms and techniques used throughout this book. I've even included some tips on page 9 to make your easy Christmas crafts even easier!

★ BASECOATING

Using a flat brush, apply at least two coats of paint to ensure solid coverage. Be sure to allow paint to dry in between coats. You can use a blow-dryer to speed up the drying process.

★ DRYBRUSHING

For this technique, use a deerfoot brush or an old "fluffy" brush and dip the bristles in a small dab of paint. Remove most of the paint from the brush on a piece of dry paper towel. You basically want a "dry brush" with just a hint of color. Gently rub the bristles on the surface area until you have achieved the desired effect. This technique is a great way to apply softly colored cheeks to your projects.

★ SPATTERING OR "FLYSPECKING"

For this technique, you use an old toothbrush to apply tiny specks of paint onto the surface area. Using a light ivory or white color allows you to create a soft, snowy look for your Christmas projects. Although some designers prefer to thin their paint with water first (approximately ⅔ paint to ⅓ water), I prefer to simply moisten the toothbrush bristles, then dip the toothbrush into a pool of paint. Remove excess paint onto a paper towel, then run your finger across the ends of the bristles, holding the toothbrush over the area to be spattered.

★ WASH

Thin a small dab of paint with water to achieve a transparent color. Apply the wash to your surface, gradually adding more coats to deepen the color to the desired shade. This technique is commonly used to antique projects and is also used to apply the cheeks onto the papier mâché North Woods Santa (see page 20).

★ DOTS AND HIGHLIGHTS

The easiest way to make dots is to dip the end of a paintbrush handle into a fresh dab of paint, then apply the tip onto your surface. Repeat this process for each dot needed.

You can vary your dot sizes by using a smaller or larger paintbrush handle. For really tiny dots, like cheek and eye highlights, I recommend using a liner brush.

★ SPONGE PAINTING

Two types of sponge-painting techniques are used in this book, but each one uses the sheets of compressed sponges that expand when moistened in water. It's important to remember that all painting should be done with a damp, not wet sponge, so be sure to squeeze the excess water from the sponge. If your sponge is too wet, the paint will bleed on your surface.

A) SURFACE TEXTURE • A damp piece of sponge can be used to apply a textured basecoat or accent color to a project. The size of the sponge you use will depend on the size of the area to be painted. You simply dip the dampened sponge into a pool of paint and apply it onto the surface of your project. You can apply additional coats as necessary.

B) PAINTING SHAPES • You can make cardboard templates (see page 54), then trace these shapes directly onto dry sheets of compressed sponge. Once you cut out the dry sponge shapes with scissors, you simply dip the dampened sponges into a pool of paint and press the shapes firmly onto the desired surface area. This technique is used to create the Three Bears Gift Bag (see page 45).

★ APPLYING SNOW TEXTURE MEDIUM

Use a palette knife to apply DecoArt Snow-Tex onto Styrofoam shapes and Delta Freshly Fallen Snow onto the Sugarplum Cottage (see page 14). However, for the smaller trims such as the evergreen sprigs and pinecones, it's much easier just to apply the snow texture medium with your fingers.

GENERAL PAINTING TIPS

• Before attempting any new painting technique, always practice first on a spare piece of paper.

• Cover your work surface with wax paper. Wax paper makes a cost-effective palette for your painting and sponge-painting techniques.

• Use a blow-dryer to speed up the drying process.

• Have a brush basin or container of clean water handy to rinse your brushes. Don't allow the paint to dry on your brush.

SPATTERING TIPS

• I always test the spatters before applying this technique or I do the backside of the project first just to be safe.

• The more water you add to your paint or to the bristles of your toothbrush, the larger and more transparent your spatters will be.

SPONGE PAINTING TIPS

• Remember that the sponge shapes will expand when moistened in water. That is why the pattern sizes are slightly smaller than the finished designs.

• Let each area dry completely before continuing on to the next step.

• Remember that sponge painting is a spontaneous process (no two designs are ever alike!). You want the look of uneven edges and unpainted holes, which adds to the simple charm of the designs.

TIPS FOR USING AIR-DRY MODELING CLAY AND INSTANT PAPIER MÂCHÉ

• Cover your work surface with wax paper or plastic wrap to prevent clay or papier mâché from sticking.

• Use warm water to facilitate mixing the papier mâché. The mixture should have the consistency of stiff cookie dough with no dry pieces. If the mixture is too moist, add more of the dry pulp. If the mixture is too dry, very sparingly add more warm water. No mixing is required for the modeling clay.

• While working on your project, keep excess clay in a resealable plastic bag and the papier mâché mixture covered with wax paper or plastic wrap to prevent dryness.

• Store unused clay and papier mâché in resealable plastic bags. Keep the unused papier mâché in the refrigerator.

• Keep a bowl of warm water handy when sculpting to keep your hands clean and moist. Hand lotion also helps with the blending and to keep the clay or papier mâché mixture from sticking to your hands.

• You may prefer to wait until the base piece is dry before adding additional features. (This is especially true when working on the papier mâché North Woods Santa.) After applying features to any of the projects, use moist fingers to blend the area onto the main form. When adding clay onto an already dried piece (e.g., adding a nose or cheeks onto a Santa face), dip your fingers in water first to moisten the clay before attaching.

• For even drying, set your project on a wire rack or grill. For the Gingerbread Boy Ornament, turn it over repeatedly to prevent the edges from curling upward.

• Use a small heater or blow-dryer to speed up the drying process.

• During the drying process, slight cracks may appear. Fill in the cracks with more clay or papier mâché and allow to dry.

• You can use a variety of household tools and objects (e.g., toothpicks, knives) to create interesting textures on your clay and papier mâché designs. To prevent the clay or papier mâché from sticking, dip modeling tools in water first. This will also prevent the clay from sticking to your cookie cutter.

• For your papier mâché projects, apply a generous coat of acrylic gesso to seal the surface prior to painting.

Visions of Sugarplums

Nothing says Christmas like the spicy scent of gingerbread baking in the oven. The sweet aroma brings us back to a simpler time when charming gingerbread cookies adorned the tree and served as festive trimmings for a cozy Christmas kitchen. And let's not forget the sheer delight of children on Christmas morning as they savor the home-baked treats tucked inside their hand-knit stockings.

If you're craving an old-fashioned country Christmas, you'll love creating this delectable array of homespun treasures—an enchanting sugarplum cottage, cookie cutter ornaments and trims, and lots of sweet surprises to brighten your home for the holidays.

So quick and easy, these irresistible delights are perfect for gift giving, and best of all, no baking is required!

GINGERBREAD BOY
Ornament

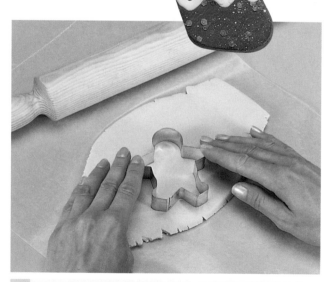

Y̶ou can almost smell the sweet fragrance of holiday baking as you craft this charming gingerbread ornament. Cleverly crafted from rolled clay and a gingerbread cookie cutter, this project is guaranteed to bring hours of festive fun! In addition to a charming Christmas tree ornament, this delightful character makes a wonderful table favor, stocking stuffer or package trim.

Materials

- paintbrushes and general supplies (see page 6)
- air-dry modeling clay (I use Creative Paperclay)
- Delta Ceramcoat acrylic paint: Raw Sienna, White, Charcoal, Cardinal Red
- Tulip White (or Scribbles Shiny White) dimensional paint
- Delta Ceramcoat matte interior varnish
- iridescent crystal glitter
- 1/2" x 4" (1cm x 10cm) strip of red/green plaid fabric
- 1/4" (6mm) gold jingle bell
- 6" (15cm) piece of miniature pine garland
- small cluster of artificial red berries
- rolling pin
- 3¼" (8cm) (tall) gingerbread boy cookie cutter
- old, worn toothbrush
- glue gun/glue sticks

1 **CUT OUT THE GINGERBREAD BOY SHAPE**

Cover your work surface with wax paper. Use the rolling pin to flatten the clay to a 1/4" (6mm) thickness. Using a cookie cutter, cut out a gingerbread boy clay shape by pressing the sharp edge of the cookie cutter through the flattened clay and removing the excess clay around the edges of the cookie cutter. Wet your fingertips with warm water and smooth the edges of the ornament. Allow to dry, turning it over frequently to prevent the sides from curling upward.

2 BASECOAT THE ORNAMENT AND APPLY TRIM

Basecoat the ornaments with Raw Sienna. Use White dimensional paint for icing trim along the head, hands and feet. Allow icing trim to dry.

3 FINISH THE ORNAMENT

Referring to the pattern on page 55, trace or freehand the features of the gingerbread boy. Use Charcoal for the eyes and White for the pupils. Drybrush the cheeks with Cardinal Red and place White dots for the cheek highlights.

Next, paint three Charcoal dots for the buttons and add two tiny White buttonholes for each. Let dry. Then, use an old, worn toothbrush to spatter the ornament with White and allow to dry. Apply matte varnish and immediately sprinkle with iridescent glitter while the varnish is still wet.

To complete the ornament, cut a fabric strip approximately ½" x 4" (1cm x 10cm) and tie a knot in the center to form a bow. Trim the ends to the desired length, and hot glue the bow above the first button. Then hot glue a gold jingle bell to the center of the bow. Lastly, cut a 6" (15cm) piece of miniature pine garland. Hot glue the ends of the garland to the back of the ornament for the hanger. For a final touch, hot glue a berry sprig to the top of the hanger.

GINGERBREAD POTPOURRI CANDLE JAR

A glass mason jar becomes an enchanting candleholder when filled with your favorite blend of potpourri and adorned with a charming gingerbread ornament—a wonderful way to light up the holidays with pure homespun charm.

Follow the directions to make one gingerbread boy ornament without the hanger. Tacky glue a cut or torn fabric strip [approximately 2½" x 13" (6cm x 33cm)] around the center of the jar, pressing to flatten any wrinkles. Then hot glue the ornament onto the fabric strip. Fill the jar with your favorite holiday potpourri and insert a glass votive candleholder and candle into the top of the jar. To complete, tie a bow using three strands of green raffia. Hot glue the bow to the rim of the jar, and hot glue a red button to the center of the bow.

SUGARPLUM *Cottage*

*V*isions of sugarplums will surely dance through your head as you create this enchanting ginger-bread cottage. With its delectable "icing" rooftop and candy trims, it looks good enough to eat! But fortunately, unlike the edible type, you can display this sweet creation in your holiday home year after year.

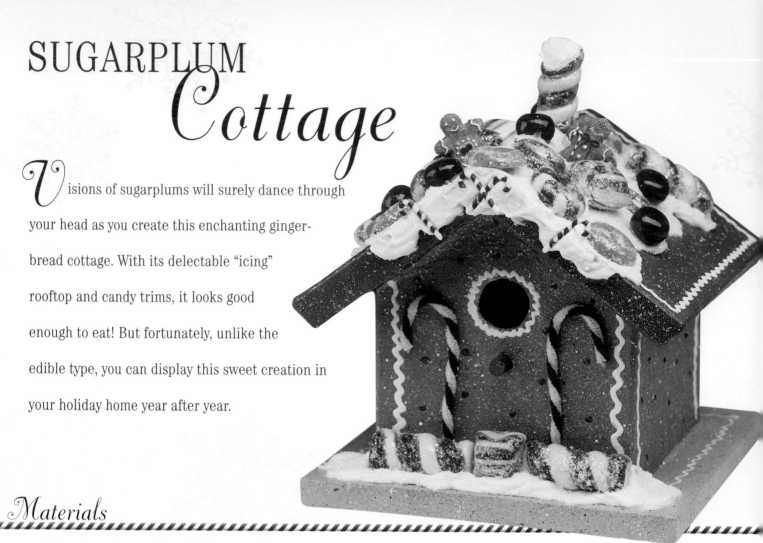

Materials

- paintbrushes and general supplies (see page 6)
- papier mâché birdhouse, 7" (18cm) base, 6½" (17cm) high
- Delta Ceramcoat acrylic paint: Golden Brown (Raw Sienna works well, too), Spice Brown, Quaker Grey, White
- Tulip White and True Red (or Scribbles Shiny White and Shiny Christmas Red) dimensional paint
- Delta Ceramcoat matte acrylic varnish
- iridescent crystal glitter
- DecoArt Glamour Dust
- two 4 fl. oz. (120ml) jars Delta Freshly Fallen Snow
- an assortment of twenty-two artificial Christmas candies (I use candies from a Christmas candy garland)
- seven large artificial red berries, approximately ⅝" (2cm)
- two 1¼" (3cm) miniature resin gingerbread ornament trims
- four 1" (3cm) miniature candy canes
- two 4" (10cm) pieces of 6mm red-and-white striped chenille stem
- old, worn toothbrush
- palette knife (or plastic knife)
- glue gun/glue sticks

1 PAINT THE BIRDHOUSE

Basecoat the house Golden Brown (or Raw Sienna), the roof Spice Brown and the base Quaker Grey. Using an old, worn toothbrush, spatter with White, then Spice Brown.

Using White dimensional paint, apply icing trim around the edges of the house (including the hole), roof and base. Apply red candy dots on the house, using True Red dimensional Paint. Allow icing trim and dots to dry. Apply matte varnish, then immediately sprinkle with iridescent crystal glitter and Glamour Dust while the varnish is still wet.

2 **APPLY SNOW TO THE ROOFTOP**

Using a palette or plastic knife, apply Freshly Fallen Snow for icing on the rooftop. Then sprinkle with iridescent crystal glitter and Glamour Dust.

3 **DECORATE THE HOUSE**

Press the artificial candies and red berries into the icing snow. Insert an artificial peppermint stick for the chimney (add more icing and glitter onto the top of the chimney). Cut the hangers off two miniature resin gingerbread ornaments and insert them into the icing on the rooftop. Press four miniature candy canes into the icing on the front edge of the roof (overlap two in the center). Allow icing snow to dry. If necessary, secure any loose candies and other trims with hot glue.

Next, apply icing snow onto the front of the base and sprinkle with iridescent crystal glitter and Glamour Dust. Add artificial candies and allow to dry.

Then, cut two 4" (10cm) pieces of red-and-white striped chenille stems. Bend one end of each stem over to form a candy cane shape. Hot glue the chenille candy cane stems onto the front of your Sugarplum Cottage.

Tip

Instead of artificial candies, use an assortment of real Christmas candies. Hard varieties such as peppermints, Life Savers or candy cane pieces would be more durable than the soft, chewy types.

SWEET HEART ORNAMENT

This heartwarming gingerbread ornament will fill your home with the simple joys of the season. Basecoat a wooden heart with Raw Sienna. (Use a precut shape or one of the patterns on page 55 to cut your own.) When dry, spatter with White, using an old, worn toothbrush. Next, apply white dimensional paint around the edges for the icing trim and allow to dry. Apply matte varnish to the heart ornament then immediately sprinkle with iridescent crystal glitter while the varnish is still wet. Hot glue two red buttons, one white button, two miniature evergreen sprigs, and three berries onto the heart. For the hanger, curl a 12" (30cm) piece of a red-and-white striped 6mm chenille stem around a wooden dowel or pencil, and hot glue the ends onto the back of the heart.

GINGERBREAD BOY *Decoration*

Simple holiday charm is the best way to describe this delightful gingerbread boy decoration. Fashioned from inexpensive kraft paper, he is adorned with homespun accents and a delectable icing trim. What a festive touch for your country kitchen!

Materials

- paintbrushes and general supplies (see page 6)
- kraft paper (heavy brown paper bags or parcel wrap)
- polyester fiberfill
- Delta Ceramcoat acrylic paint: Raw Sienna, Charcoal, White, Cardinal Red
- Tulip White (or Scribbles Shiny White) dimensional paint
- Delta Ceramcoat matte interior varnish
- iridescent crystal glitter
- 1" x 5" (3cm x 13cm) red/green homespun plaid fabric strip
- $^3/_8$" (10mm) gold jingle bell
- two 1" (3cm) square fabric patches (red/green homespun plaid)
- $^1/_2$"–$^5/_8$" (1cm–2cm) buttons: three brown, one green or red
- 1$^1/_2$" x $^3/_4$" (4cm x 2cm) primitive wooden heart
- 13" (33cm) miniature pine garland
- three artificial red berries
- old, worn toothbrush
- glue gun/glue sticks

Tip

If you plan to make several gingerbread boy decorations, transfer the shape onto a piece of lightweight cardboard or posterboard and cut it out. Use the cutout as a template instead of hand-transferring the shape with tracing paper each time.

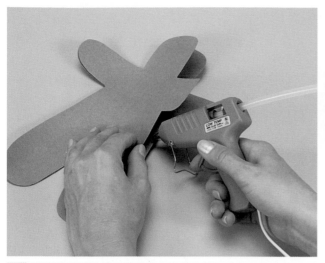

1 CUT OUT TWO SHAPES AND GLUE THE LEGS

Referring to the pattern on page 55, use a pencil to trace the ginger-bread boy shape onto tracing paper. Slip a piece of transfer paper underneath the tracing paper and, with a pencil or ballpoint pen, draw the gingerbread boy pattern twice onto kraft paper (or a brown paper bag). Cut out each gingerbread boy shape.

Next, line up the edges of the two gingerbread boys. Hot glue the inside edges of the legs together, leaving the arm and head areas open to stuff fiberfill once the gingerbread boy is painted.

2 PAINT THE GINGERBREAD BOY

Basecoat the gingerbread boy with Raw Sienna and allow to dry. Use White dimensional paint for the icing trim around the head, hands and feet. Let dry.

Next, paint the face, referring to the pattern on page 55. Use Charcoal for the eyebrows and eyes, and White for the pupils. For the cheeks, drybrush with Cardinal Red and place White dots for the cheek highlights. Allow to dry.

Then, spatter the gingerbread boy with White, using an old, worn toothbrush. When dry, apply matte varnish to the gingerbread boy, then immediately sprinkle with iridescent crystal glitter while the varnish is still wet.

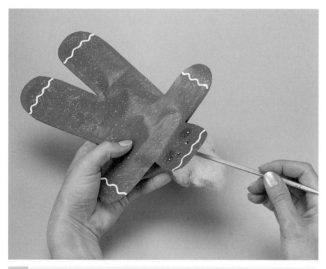

3 INSERT THE POLYESTER FIBERFILL

Use the tip of a paintbrush handle to stuff the leg area with small pieces of polyester fiberfill. Once the legs are stuffed, hot glue the inside edges of one arm. Then stuff the arm with fiberfill. Continue for the second arm and finally the head.

4 ADD THE FINAL TOUCHES

Next, cut a piece of fabric approximately 1" x 5" (3cm x 13cm). Tie a knot in the center to form a bow. Trim the ends of the bow to the desired length and hot glue it onto the neck area. Then, hot glue the jingle bell onto the center of the bow.

Cut two 1" (3cm) square fabric patches and hot glue them onto the lower right leg, overlapping the edges slightly. Then hot glue a green or red button onto the center of the patches. Hot glue the three brown buttons onto the front center of the body.

Next, paint the wooden heart Cardinal Red. Use the toothbrush to spatter the heart with White. Outline the edges of the heart with White dimensional paint. Allow to dry. Apply matte varnish and sprinkle with glitter. When dry, hot glue the wooden heart onto the gingerbread boy.

Finally, cut a 13" (33cm) piece of miniature pine garland. Hot glue the ends of the garland to the back of the gingerbread boy for a hanger. Then hot glue three artificial red berries onto the pine garland hanger.

Santa Claus Lane

*L*ike most people, I simply adore Christmas. It's that one time of year when we wear our merry elf hats and transform our holiday homes into a magical wonderland of yuletide treasures. And for me, it just wouldn't be Christmas without my cheery collection of Santas filling every nook and cranny of our home.

One of the greatest joys in Santa collecting is finding creative and innovative ways to recycle everyday household items into charming gifts and decorating delights. As you stroll down Santa Claus Lane, you'll discover how an old mason jar, brown paper bags, even plain drinking cups and glass ornaments can play the starring role of this legendary gift-bearer in your Christmas celebrations.

From quick and easy Santa ornaments and favors, to more elaborate gifts and decorations—you're sure to capture the joy and magic of the season as you celebrate the many faces of Old St. Nick.

NORTH WOODS *Santa*

I love creating papier mâché Santas, so I couldn't resist sharing one of my favorite designs! Inspired by the rustic beauty of the North Woods, this exquisite fellow gathers nature's treasures as he strolls through the wintry forest. With flurries in the forecast, he makes sure to pack his snowshoes for his long journey ahead.

Materials

- paintbrushes and general supplies (see page 6)
- 8" (20cm) Styrofoam ball
- 4" (10cm) Styrofoam ball
- round wooden toothpick
- instant papier mâché (I use Celluclay Instant Papier Mâché)
- white acrylic gesso
- FolkArt Apple Spice acrylic paint (or Delta Ceramcoat: mixture of Sonoma Wine and Tomato Spice)
- Delta Ceramcoat acrylic paint: Charcoal, Light Ivory, Fleshtone, Spice Brown
- Delta Ceramcoat matte interior varnish
- DecoArt Glamour Dust
- iridescent crystal glitter
- DecoArt Snow-Tex
- pair of 4" (10cm) long miniature snowshoes
- artificial pine spray
- ten to twelve small to medium pinecones
- three small pieces of birch bark or twigs
- Rusty Tin-Tiques accents, 2¾" x 2¼" (7cm x 6cm) moose, 2" (5cm) star and 3" (8cm) tree
- clusters of artificial red berries
- small sprigs of statice
- sharp knife
- old, worn toothbrush
- glue gun/glue sticks

1 ASSEMBLE THE SANTA

Using a sharp knife, cut a sliver off the bottom of the 8" (20cm) Styrofoam ball so it stands upright. Press the bottom of the 4" (10cm) ball onto a hard surface to flatten slightly. Insert a wooden toothpick halfway through the top center of the 8" (20cm) ball. Apply plenty of hot glue onto the area around the toothpick then immediately press the bottom (flat side) of the 4" (10cm) ball through the toothpick to form the head. Allow the form to set.

2 | PREPARE THE PAPIER MÂCHÉ

Mix the papier mâché with warm water following the manufacturer's instructions. Knead the mixture until it is smooth and has the consistency of cookie dough. I find it easier to mix the papier mâché in a mixing bowl rather than in a plastic bag. (For other great tips on working with papier mâché, please see page 9.)

Tip

Keep a bowl of warm water handy to moisten your fingers to make blending easier.

3 | APPLY THE PAPIER MÂCHÉ

Cover your work surface with wax paper. Use your fingers to apply the papier mâché mixture onto the Santa form. Dip your fingers in a bowl of warm water to moisten, then blend the edges until smooth. Place the form on a drying rack and allow to dry. You can also use a blow-dryer to speed up the drying process.

4 | FORM THE HAT

Apply papier mâché onto the top of the head to form the hat. Blend the edges until smooth.

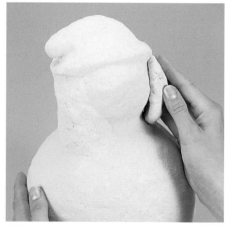

7 | FORM THE BEARD

Press papier mâché around the sides of the head for the hair and in front to form the beard, blending around the face.

5 | APPLY THE FUR TRIM

For the fur trim, form a ¾" (2cm) wide coil of papier mâché and press it around the bottom of the hat. Blend the edges until smooth.

6 | ADD THE POM-POM

For the pom-pom, form a ¾" (2cm) ball of papier mâché and press it onto the tip of the hat until secure. Blend the edges until smooth.

8 TEXTURE THE BEARD

For a smoother beard, continue to blend the surface. For a more textured beard, use your fingers to form indents. For a different textured effect, you can use a knife to add ridges. Antiquing with a wash of Spice Brown will bring out the texture once you begin the painting process (see step 13).

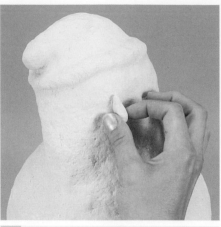

9 FORM THE NOSE

For the nose, form a 1/2" (1cm) ball of papier mâché into a triangular shape and press it onto the center of the face, just above the beard. Blend the edges until smooth.

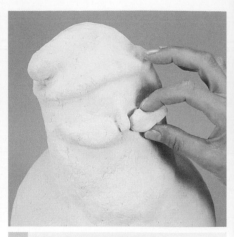

10 ADD THE MUSTACHE

For the mustache, form two 3/4" (2cm) balls of papier mâché into mustache shapes and press them onto the face on each side of the nose. Blend the edges until smooth.

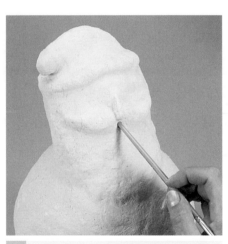

11 INDENT TO FORM THE MOUTH

For the mouth, use the round edge of a paintbrush handle to indent the area in the center of the mustache, just under the nose.

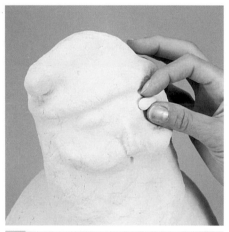

12 FORM THE EYEBROWS

For the eyebrows, form two 3/8" (10mm) balls and roll them slightly between your fingers. Press them onto the face area just under the fur trim of the hat. Blend the edges until smooth and allow all the facial features to dry.

13 SEAL AND PAINT THE SANTA

Apply a generous coat of white acrylic gesso to the Santa form. The gesso will seal the surface to enhance paint adhesion.

After the gesso is dry, basecoat the body and hat with FolkArt Apple Spice (or you can use a mixture of Delta Ceramcoat Sonoma Wine and Tomato Spice).

Paint the buttons Charcoal with Light Ivory buttonholes. For the hair, beard, mustache, fur trim and pom-pom, use Light Ivory. Next, basecoat the face with Fleshtone and allow to dry.

Paint the eyes Charcoal with Light Ivory pupils and tiny Light Ivory highlights. For the cheeks, use a wash of Apple Spice and add a Light Ivory cheek highlight. Paint the eyebrows Light Ivory and the mouth Fleshtone, accented with a wash of Apple Spice.

To finish painting the Santa, antique it with a wash of Spice Brown. Then, using an old, worn toothbrush, spatter the Santa with Light Ivory and allow to dry. Next, apply matte varnish. While the varnish is still wet, sprinkle with Glamour Dust and iridescent crystal glitter.

14 APPLY SNOW-TEX TO THE TRIMS

Apply Snow-Tex to the snowshoes, pine spray, pinecones and birch bark pieces (or twigs).

15 HOT GLUE THE SHOULDER TRIMS

Hot glue the pine spray, snowshoes, pinecones, rusty tin accents (moose, star and tree), berries, statice, and birch bark (or twigs) to the shoulder area of the Santa.

NORTH WOODS GRAPEVINE WREATH

Create the perfect setting for your North Woods Santa. To display, set the Santa inside a decorated garland for a real woodsy touch. Simply cut off approximately 36" (91cm) from a grapevine garland and overlap the ends to form a circular wreath. Secure with a piece of general-purpose wire. Apply Snow-Tex to the garland and pinecones. Hot glue pinecones, berries and statice onto the garland.

OLD-WORLD SANTA
Stocking

*F*illed with holiday greenery and other woodsy trims, this kraft paper Santa stocking will add a touch of old-world charm to your Christmas décor. The Santa face, which is sculpted from a Styrofoam egg base and Paperclay air-dry clay, also makes a wonderful ornament when hung with an elastic cord hanger.

Materials

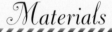

- paintbrushes and general supplies (see page 6)
- 3" (8cm) Styrofoam egg
- air-dry modeling clay (I use Creative Paperclay)
- kraft paper (heavy brown paper bags or parcel wrap)
- Delta Ceramcoat acrylic paint: Fleshtone, Tomato Spice, Charcoal, Light Ivory, Dark Forest Green, Burnt Umber (optional), Straw
- Delta Ceramcoat matte interior spray varnish
- DecoArt Snow-Tex
- natural wool doll hair (see Resources page 61)
- 1¼"–1½" (3cm–4cm) miniature woodlets: one star, two trees
- two 1" (3cm) square fabric patches
- ½" (1cm) button (red, green or white)
- polyester fiberfill
- woodsy trims: one 15" x 9" (38cm x 23cm) pine spray, three pinecones, five red berries, birch bark pieces or branches, statice
- two 1"–1½" (3cm–4cm) miniature evergreen sprigs (cut from garland)
- three artificial red berries
- 42" (1m) 18-gauge general-purpose wire
- three strands natural raffia
- 2" (5cm) Rusty Tin-Tiques star
- sharp knife
- old, worn toothbrush
- sharp scissors (or wire cutters)
- ⅜" (10cm) wooden dowel
- glue gun/glue sticks

NATURAL WOOL DOLL HAIR

Curly Crepe craft hair in white and Wavy Wool in natural work great for Santa's hair, beard and mustache. See the Resources section on page 61 for more information.

1 APPLY MODELING CLAY

Use a sharp knife to cut a 3" (8cm) Styrofoam egg lengthwise in equal halves to form the base of Santa's head. You will need only one-half of the egg.

Cover work surface with wax paper. Apply air-dry modeling clay to the surface of the Styrofoam base. Please refer to the pattern on page 56 for the basic facial shape.

2 FORM THE NOSE

For the nose, form a ³⁄₈" (10mm) ball of air-dry modeling clay and press it onto the center of the face. Dip your fingers in a bowl of warm water to moisten, then blend the edges of the nose until smooth.

3 ADD THE CHEEKS

For the cheeks, form two ¹⁄₂" (1cm) balls of air-dry modeling clay and press onto each side of the nose. Blend the edges of the cheeks until smooth. Allow the Santa face to dry.

4 PAINT THE SANTA FACE

First, basecoat the face with a mixture of Fleshtone and a few drops of Tomato Spice. The Tomato Spice gives the basecoat a rosy tone. Let dry.

Next, paint the eyes Charcoal and use Light Ivory for the pupils. For the cheeks, drybrush with Tomato Spice and add cheek highlights using Light Ivory. Apply matte varnish and allow to dry.

5 HOT GLUE THE WOOL HAIR →

Hot glue the wool doll hair for Santa's hair, beard and mustache. Use your fingers to fluff the wool into the desired shape.

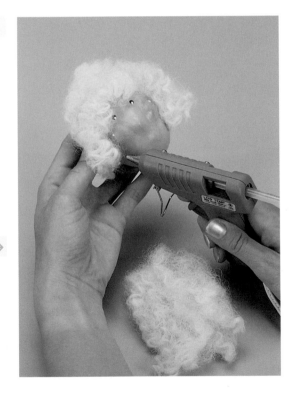

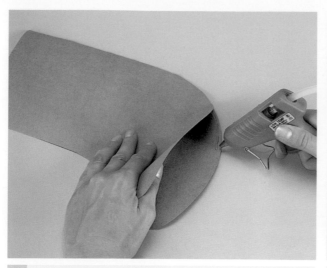

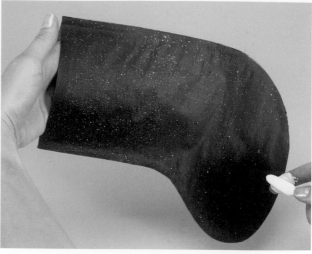

6 MAKE THE STOCKING

Referring to the pattern on page 57, use a pencil to trace the stocking shape onto tracing paper. Slip a piece of transfer paper underneath the tracing paper and, with a pencil or ballpoint pen, draw two stocking shapes onto kraft paper (or a brown paper bag). Cut out the two paper stockings. (For more information on using patterns, see page 54.)

Line up the edges of the two paper stockings and hot glue the inside edges together, leaving the top completely open to stuff fiberfill and woodsy trims later in step 8.

7 PAINT THE STOCKING

Basecoat the stocking with Tomato Spice. (You can basecoat the stocking in a different color if you'd like. I like to use Tomato Spice, Dark Forest Green and Light Ivory for my stockings.) Let dry.

Next, use an old, worn toothbrush to spatter the stocking with Light Ivory. (If you use Dark Forest Green as the basecoat, spatter the stocking with Light Ivory. If you use Light Ivory as the basecoat, spatter the stocking with Burnt Umber.) Allow to dry. Apply matte varnish to the stocking.

8 FINISH THE STOCKING

Paint the woodlet trims, using Straw for the star and Dark Forest Green for the trees. Let dry. Then spatter with Light Ivory and allow to dry. Next, apply matte varnish.

Hot glue the woodlet trims onto the top of the stocking and the Santa head onto the center of the stocking. Next, cut two 1" (3cm) fabric patches and hot glue them onto the toe of the stocking, slightly overlapping the edges. Hot glue a red, green or white button in the center of the fabric patches.

When the outside of the stocking is completed, stuff the inside of the stocking with polyester fiberfill. Use the tip of a paintbrush handle to push the fiberfill into hard-to-reach areas.

Tip

If you plan to make several stockings, I find it saves time to transfer the pattern onto a piece of lightweight cardboard or posterboard. Once this cardboard template is cut out, you can use it over and over again to trace your pattern.

9 **APPLY SNOW-TEX TO THE TRIMS**

Using your fingers or a palette knife, apply Snow-Tex to the following woodsy trims: pine spray, pinecones and birch bark pieces (or branches). Hot glue the woodsy trims, red berries and statice inside the stocking.

Next, cut two 1"–1½" (3cm–4cm) miniature evergreen sprigs. Apply Snow-Tex to the sprigs then hot glue the sprigs to the Santa head. Hot glue three red berries onto the evergreen sprigs.

This charming Santa plays the "starring" role to complete your old-world holiday décor. Follow the directions to make an Old-World Santa head. Decorate a grape-vine star with a variety of woodsy trims, red berries and statice. Hot glue the Santa head onto the center of the star and add a wire hanger, raffia bow and homespun trims.

10 **ADD A WIRE HANGER**

Create a wire hanger to hang your stocking. Use sharp scissors (or wire cutters) to cut 42" (1m) of 18-gauge general-purpose wire. Wrap the wire piece tightly around a wooden dowel to curl. Insert the ends of the wire hanger through each side of the stocking and twist the ends to secure. It may be necessary to stretch the wire hanger somewhat to fit over the trims inside the stocking.

Next, tie a bow at the top of the hanger using three strands of natural raffia. Use scissors to trim the ends to the desired length. Secure the bow with hot glue if necessary. Then hot glue the 2" (5cm) tin star to the center of the raffia bow, adding the finishing touch to your Old-World Santa Stocking.

SANTA *Cookie Jar*

Everyone knows Santa loves cookies! And with that in mind, we created this charming Santa cookie jar to brighten your holiday kitchen. Crafted from an old-fashioned mason jar and embellished with an assortment of homespun trims, he's sure to delight children of all ages.

Materials

- paintbrushes and general supplies (see page 6)
- glass mason jar (quart size) with lid
- spray primer (or basecoat with acrylic gesso)
- Delta Ceramcoat acrylic paint: Cardinal Red, Light Ivory, Fleshtone, Charcoal, Dark Forest Green
- fine-point black permanent pen (Pigma Micron 05 or Zig Memory System 05)
- Delta Ceramcoat matte interior spray varnish
- 3/4" (2cm) wooden button
- 3/8" (10mm) wooden button
- two miniature resin gingerbread ornament trims, 1 1/4" (3cm)
- 12" (30cm) piece of miniature evergreen garland (size to fit around top of jar)
- eight 3/8" (10mm) gold jingle bells
- two small fabric patches, approximately 3/4" x 1/2" (2cm x 1cm)
- old, worn toothbrush
- glue gun/glue sticks

1 PREPARE THE JAR

Spray the jar and lid with primer or apply a coat of gesso to enable the paint to adhere to the glass surface of the jar. Then basecoat the jar and lid with Cardinal Red and let dry. Paint the rim Light Ivory.

2 PAINT THE SANTA FACE

To paint the facial features, refer to the pattern on page 56. Paint the face Fleshtone; the hair, beard and mustache Light Ivory; the eyes Charcoal; the pupils Light Ivory; the eyebrows Light Ivory. Drybrush the cheeks with Cardinal Red and paint the cheek highlights Light Ivory. Outline the hair, beard, mustache and mouth with a black permanent pen.

3 FINISH PAINTING THE JAR

Randomly paint large Light Ivory dots on the jar. Around each large dot, paint three smaller dots using Dark Forest Green. Then paint a 3/4" (2cm) wooden button Light Ivory for the jar handle and a 3/8" (10mm) wooden button

Cardinal Red for the nose. Add a dot of Light Ivory for a highlight.

Next, use an old, worn toothbrush to spatter the jar, lid and button nose with Light Ivory and let dry. Then apply matte varnish to the jar, lid and two wooden buttons.

4 ADD THE FINISHING TOUCHES

Hot glue the lid onto the jar, then hot glue the Light Ivory button onto the center of the lid. For the nose, hot glue the Cardinal Red button onto the face.

Cut the hangers off two miniature gingerbread ornaments and hot glue them under Santa's beard on the front of the jar. Next, cut a 12" (30cm) piece of miniature evergreen garland (the length may vary depending on the size of the jar opening) and hot glue it around the rim. Then, hot glue eight gold jingle bells around the evergreen garland. Finally, hot glue two small fabric patches on the top of the lid.

SANTA GLASS BALL ORNAMENT

MATERIALS: PAINTBRUSHES AND GENERAL SUPPLIES (SEE PAGE 6) • 2⅝" (7cm) glass ball ornament • Delta Ceramcoat acrylic paint: Cardinal Red, Fleshtone, Light Ivory, Charcoal • Delta Ceramcoat matte interior varnish • iridescent crystal glitter • 7" (8cm) miniature pine garland • three artificial red berries • small pieces of sponge • old, worn toothbrush • glue gun/glue sticks. **OPTIONAL:** gold curling ribbon.

1 First remove the hanger from the ornament. Then, using a small piece of dampened sponge, apply Cardinal Red paint onto the surface of the glass ball and allow to dry. Apply multiple coats as needed. **2** Referring to the pattern on page 56, use a tiny piece of sponge to apply Fleshtone paint in an oval shape for the face and let dry. Then use a small piece of sponge to apply Light Ivory paint for the hair and beard. **3** Next, paint the facial features, using Light Ivory for the mustache, Cardinal Red for the nose, Light Ivory for the nose highlight, Charcoal for the eyes, Light Ivory for the pupils, Light Ivory for the eyebrows, and Charcoal for the mouth. Then drybrush the cheeks with Cardinal Red and add a Light Ivory cheek highlight dot. **4** Use an old, worn toothbrush to spatter the ornament with Light Ivory and let dry. Apply matte varnish and immediately sprinkle with iridescent crystal glitter while the varnish is still wet. Allow to dry. **5** Next, apply matte varnish to a 7" (18cm) piece of pine garland and berries and immediately sprinkle with glitter, then let dry. Hot glue the miniature garland around the top of the ornament. Then hot glue the berries onto the front of the garland. Insert the hanger and accent with gold curling ribbon.

SANTA CANDY FAVOR CUP

MATERIALS: PAINTBRUSHES AND GENERAL SUPPLIES (SEE PAGE 6) • white plastic drinking cup, approximately 4¼" (11cm) high, 3½" (9cm) diameter at the top • Delta Ceramcoat acrylic paint: Cardinal Red, Fleshtone, Light Ivory, Charcoal, Seminole Green • Delta Ceramcoat matte interior spray varnish • three 12" (30cm) 6mm chenille stems: red, green, white or red-and-white striped • paper shredding • small pieces of sponge • old, worn toothbrush • glue gun/glue sticks.

1 Use a small piece of dampened sponge to apply Cardinal Red paint onto the entire surface of the cup, including the inside. Apply additional coats to obtain solid coverage.
2 Referring to the pattern on page 56, use a tiny piece of sponge to apply Fleshtone in an oval shape for the face and let dry. Use a sponge to apply Light Ivory for the hair and beard. Paint the mustache Light Ivory, the nose Cardinal Red, the nose highlight Light Ivory, the eyes Charcoal, the pupils Light Ivory, the eyebrows Light Ivory, and the mouth Charcoal. Drybrush the cheeks with Cardinal Red, then use Light Ivory for the highlights. **3** Using Seminole Green, paint two ivy leaves in Santa's hair. Add three tiny Cardinal Red dots for berries. Next, randomly paint Light Ivory dots around the cup and let dry. Then spatter the cup with Light Ivory. Apply matte varnish. **4** Finally, cut and hot glue two chenille: one 11" (28cm) piece of stem around the top of the cup and one 8¼" (21cm) piece of stem around the bottom. Hot glue a 12" (30cm) chenille stem inside the cup for the handle, and fill with shredded paper and your favorite candies.

Frosty Fun

With a twinkle in his eye, Jack Frost spreads his wintry magic and transforms the autumn landscape into an icy splendor. Glistening snowflakes, pearly icicles and fun-loving snowmen—it's time to bundle up in your warmest woolies and get ready for some frosty fun!

You'll discover a winter wonderland of snowy delights, a storybook world where jolly snowmen ski down blankets of freshly fallen snow and frolic among the snow-dusted pines. Although these chilly chums never melt, they're guaranteed to warm those frosty winter nights with their cheerful holiday smiles.

And even if you're only dreaming of a white Christmas, you can still bring the frosty fun of a snowy winter day indoors by creating this magical collection of icy treasures. In a twinkling, your holiday home will sparkle with wintry charm.

SNOWFLAKE MEMORY *Wreath*

*C*apture your most cherished holiday memories with photos of Christmases past, tucked among the branches of this exquisite wreath. Glistening snowflake ornaments are adorned with copies of your favorite photos and trimmed with a sparkly tinsel stem. Strands of silver beads, glittered berry sprigs and frosty foliage enhance its icy splendor. A gracefully draped snowflake ribbon adds the perfect touch of wintry elegance.

Materials

- general supplies (see page 6)
- 20" (51cm) pine wreath
- eight photos to fit in circle template (see pattern, page 58)
- eight 3¹/₂" (9cm) glittered snowflake ornaments (I use four white and four silver)
- eight 7¹/₄" (18cm) pieces of 6mm silver tinsel stems
- three yards (3m) of 2" (5cm) wide silver metallic wired ribbon (I use one with a snowflake motif)
- 9' (3m) of ¹/₂" (1cm) silver bead garland
- five miniature silver foil package trims, one 1¹/₂" (4cm) and four 1" (3cm)
- assorted floral trims: eight 2¹/₂"–3" (6cm–8cm) glittered leaves, clusters of artificial white berries, silver glittered pine foliage, sixteen silver glittered berries cut off sprigs
- compass (optional) to draw the circle
- tacky glue
- glue gun/glue sticks

CREATING A BEAUTIFUL MEMORY WREATH

1. Black-and-white photos add a nostalgic look and complement the colors of the white and silver trims.

2. Make copies at your local print shop to preserve your original photos.

3. Choose photos with a Christmas or wintry theme.

1 PREPARE THE PHOTOGRAPHS

Referring to the circle pattern (see page 58), use a pencil to trace the circle onto tracing paper.

Slip a piece of transfer paper underneath the tracing paper and, with a pencil or ballpoint pen, draw the circle pattern onto a piece of lightweight cardboard or poster-board. Use scissors to cut out the cardboard circle.

To preserve your original photos, have them photocopied at your local print shop. Bring the circle template with you so you can have your photos reduced or enlarged so that the main subject matter will fit into the circular shape. (I used black-and-white photos for a vintage look.)

2 TRACE THE CIRCLE TEMPLATE

Place the cardboard circle template onto the desired area of each photo and trace around the edges with a pencil, making sure your main image is inside the circle. Cut out the circular photo shape.

Tip

Instead of transferring the circle pattern with the tracing and transfer papers, you can use a compass to draw the circle shape directly onto the cardboard.

3 CREATE THE ORNAMENT

Use tacky glue to attach the eight circular photos onto the center of each snowflake ornament. Press the photos firmly on the edges until the glue sets to prevent the edges of the photos from curling upward.

4 ADD A TINSEL STEM BORDER

Cut eight 7¼" (18cm) pieces of silver tinsel stems. Hot glue the edges to form circular shapes and let set. Then hot glue the circular tinsel stems around the edges of the photos.

5 DECORATE THE WREATH

Once your photo ornaments are completed, it's time to decorate the wreath. Wrap the three yards (3m) of wired ribbon around a 20" (51cm) wreath. Secure with hot glue.

Cut 1' (30cm) off the 9' (3m) silver bead garland; you need only 8' (2m). Wrap the silver bead garland around the wreath and secure with hot glue. Then hot glue the eight photo snowflake ornaments onto the wreath.

Next, add the remaining embellishments. Hot glue the miniature foil packages onto the wreath, gluing one 1½" (4cm) package and two 1" (3cm) packages together in one cluster. Hot glue the remaining 1" (3cm) packages separately. For the finishing touch, hot glue the assorted floral trims (glittered leaves, white berry clusters, silver glittered foliage and silver glittered berries).

CHILLY *Chum*

*T*his jolly egg snowman is ready to hit the slopes on a blanket of fresh-fallen snow. For a charming wintry setting, display your chilly chum with miniature frosted Christmas trees on a blanket of fleece batting or sprinkled synthetic snowflakes. You can even craft more of these roly-poly snow pals in a variety of sizes to create your very own snowman collection.

Materials

- paintbrushes and general supplies (see page 6)
- 6" (15cm) Styrofoam egg
- air-dry modeling clay (I use Creative Paperclay)
- Delta Ceramcoat acrylic paint: Charcoal, Light Ivory, Cardinal Red, Dark Goldenrod,
- DecoArt Snow-Tex
- Delta Ceramcoat matte interior varnish
- DecoArt Glamour Dust
- iridescent crystal glitter
- two 2¹⁄₂" (6cm) twigs for arms
- strip of red/green plaid fabric, approximately 1" x 5" (3cm x 13cm)
- ³⁄₈" (10mm) gold jingle bell
- 8" (20cm) miniature evergreen garland
- 3" (8cm) black felt hat; brim is approximately 3" wide x 3¹⁄₂" long (8cm x 9cm)
- three artificial red berries
- set of miniature decorative skis with poles, approximately 6¹⁄₂" (17cm) (see Specialty Resources on page 62)
- palette knife
- glue gun/glue sticks

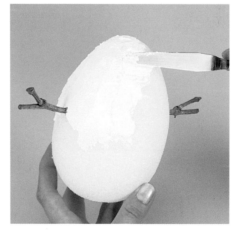

1 CREATE THE SNOWMAN BODY

Firmly press the bottom (large end) of the Styrofoam egg against a hard surface to flatten slightly. (This will make it easier to glue the egg snowman onto the wooden skis in step 4.)

Next, insert a twig approximately ³⁄₄" (2cm) into each side of the egg for the arms. Remove the twigs, and apply hot glue into each hole. Reinsert each twig arm and allow the glue to set.

Use a palette knife to apply Snow-Tex to cover the surface of the Styrofoam egg. Allow to dry.

2 PAINT THE FACE

Referring to the pattern on page 58, paint the eyes and mouth Charcoal and the pupils Light Ivory. For the cheeks, either drybrush with Cardinal Red or brush on pink powdered blush for a softer look. When dry, apply matte varnish to the snowman form. While the varnish is still wet, sprinkle with Glamour Dust and iridescent crystal glitter. Let dry.

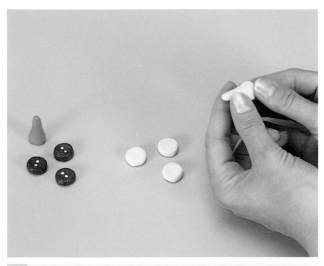

Cut a piece of red/green plaid fabric approximately 1" x 5" (3cm x 13cm). Tie a knot in the center to form a bow. Trim the ends to the desired length and hot glue the bow just above the top button. Then hot glue a $^3/_8$" (10mm) gold jingle bell into the center of the bow.

Next, cut an 8" (20cm) piece of miniature evergreen garland. Apply Snow-Tex to the garland and the black felt hat. Hot glue the evergreen garland and three berries onto the brim of the hat. Then hot glue the hat onto the top of the snowman.

To finish, apply Snow-Tex onto the twig arms, wooden skis and poles. Hot glue the skis onto the bottom of the snowman. Set the ski poles onto the twig arms. Or glue him to a small wooden sled and head for the hills!

3 FORM THE NOSE AND BUTTONS

Next, form a $^1/_2$"–$^5/_8$" (1cm–2cm) ball of air-dry modeling clay and roll it into a carrot shape for the nose. For the buttons, form three $^1/_2$" (1cm) balls of clay and then flatten slightly. Allow both nose and buttons to dry before painting the nose Dark Goldenrod and the buttons Charcoal with Light Ivory buttonholes. Apply varnish to the nose and buttons, then immediately sprinkle lightly with Glamour Dust while the varnish is still wet. Hot glue the nose and buttons onto the snowman when dry.

JOLLY EGG
SNOWMAN ORNAMENT

Let this frosty fellow add wintry fun to your tree-trimming celebrations. Follow the directions to make a Chilly Chum (without skis), using a 3" (8cm) Styrofoam egg; 2" (5cm) twigs; $^3/_4$" x 4" (2cm x 10cm) piece of plaid fabric (for a bow); 6mm gold jingle bell (for the bow), 2" (5cm) hat; and $^3/_8$" (10mm) and $^1/_4$" (6mm) balls of clay to form the nose and buttons, respectively. Hot glue an evergreen sprig and one red berry to the hat. For the hanger, wrap wire around a dowel to curl it. Attach the wire to the twigs. Add a raffia bow and plastic snowflake to decorate the hanger.

SNOWMAN SNOWFLAKE
Ornament

Snowmen and snowflakes—what a delightful combination! And oh, what fun it is to create these magical keepsake ornaments. A sparkling snowflake ornament is dressed up in icy splendor, complete with miniature snowflake trims, a merry little snowman and a winter white bow. Guaranteed to melt your heart for the holidays.

Materials

- paintbrushes and general supplies (see page 6)
- 2" (5cm) Styrofoam ball
- air-dry modeling clay (I use Creative Paperclay)
- 6½" (17cm) clear acrylic snowflake ornament (see Specialty Resources on page 62)
- Delta Ceramcoat acrylic paint: Dark Goldenrod, Charcoal, Light Ivory, Cardinal Red
- DecoArt Snow-Tex
- Delta Ceramcoat matte interior varnish
- iridescent crystal glitter
- DecoArt Glamour Dust
- six ¾"–1" (2cm–3cm) miniature snowflake ornaments (remove hangers)
- 12" (30cm) of ³⁄₁₆"–¼" (5mm–6mm) wide white satin ribbon
- sharp knife
- palette knife
- glue gun/glue sticks

1 PREPARE THE SNOWMAN FACE

Use a sharp knife to cut a Styrofoam ball in half to form the base of the snowman's head. You will need only one-half of the ball for each ornament.

Use a palette knife to apply the Snow-Tex to cover the surface of the Styrofoam base. Allow to dry.

2 FORM THE NOSE

For the nose, form a ³⁄₈" (10mm) ball of clay and roll it into a carrot shape. Allow to dry.

When dry, paint the nose Dark Goldenrod and let dry. Next, apply matte varnish and sprinkle with iridescent crystal glitter and Glamour Dust while the varnish is still wet. Set the nose aside.

3 PAINT THE SNOWMAN FACE

Paint the face by referring to the pattern on page 58. Use the following colors: Charcoal for the eyes, Light Ivory for the pupils and Charcoal for the mouth. For the cheeks, drybrush Cardinal Red and use Light Ivory for the cheek highlights. (For a softer look on the cheeks, you can substitute pink powdered blush for the Cardinal Red.) Let dry.

4 FINISH THE SNOWMAN FACE

Apply matte varnish to the snowman face. While wet, sprinkle with Glamour Dust and iridescent glitter and let dry.

Next, hot glue the nose onto the center of the face.

5 HOT GLUE THE SNOWMAN FACE

Hot glue the snowman face onto the center of the 6½" (17cm) acrylic snowflake ornament. Be sure the ornament hanger is at the top.

6 ADD THE FINISHING TOUCHES

Hot glue the miniature snowflake ornaments onto the outer edges of the larger snowflake. Next, cut a 12" (30cm) piece of white ribbon. Tie a bow, then trim the ends to the desired length. Hot glue the bow directly underneath the face.

POTTED SNOW PAL

MATERIALS: PAINTBRUSHES AND GENERAL SUPPLIES (SEE PAGE 6) • 4" (10cm) clay pot • air-dry modeling clay • Delta Ceramcoat acrylic paint: White, Charcoal, Cardinal Red, Dark Goldenrod • Delta Ceramcoat matte interior varnish • DecoArt Glamour Dust • iridescent crystal glitter • DecoArt Snow-Tex • red/green plaid fabric strip, approximately $^{3}/_{4}$" x 4" (2cm x 10cm) • $^{3}/_{8}$" (10mm) gold jingle bell • two evergreen sprigs, approximately $1^{1}/_{4}$" (3cm) cut from miniature garland • four artificial red berries • three Styrofoam balls, one 2" (5cm) and two $1^{1}/_{2}$" (4cm) • seven to nine small- to medium-size pinecones • palette knife • glue gun/glue sticks.

1 Basecoat the clay pot with White and the rim Charcoal. Refer to the pattern on page 58 for the facial features. Paint the face using the following colors: Charcoal for the eyes, eyebrows and mouth; White for the pupils. For the cheeks, drybrush with Cardinal Red. Apply matte varnish to the pot, and immediately sprinkle with Glamour Dust and iridescent crystal glitter while the varnish is still wet. Let dry. **2** For the nose, form a $^{1}/_{2}$"–$^{5}/_{8}$" (1cm–2cm) ball of clay and roll into a carrot shape. Allow to dry. Paint the nose Dark Goldenrod. Apply varnish to the nose, then sprinkle lightly with Glamour Dust while the varnish is still wet. Hot glue the nose onto the snowman. **3** Form a knotted bow using a $^{3}/_{4}$" x 4" (2cm x 10cm) piece of red/green plaid fabric and trim the ends. Hot glue it below the mouth, then hot glue a jingle bell onto its center. Cut two $1^{1}/_{4}$" (3cm) pieces of miniature evergreen garland, apply Snow-Tex and hot glue onto the rim. Hot glue a red berry onto the evergreen sprigs. Apply Snow-Tex to the Styrofoam balls and let dry. Apply matte varnish. While wet, sprinkle with Glamour Dust and iridescent crystal glitter. Apply Snow-Tex to the pinecones. Hot glue the pinecones, snowballs and three red berries into the pot.

SNOWFLAKE STAR BOX

MATERIALS: PAINTBRUSHES AND GENERAL SUPPLIES (SEE PAGE 6) • papier mâché star box with lid approximately 10" x 4" (25cm x 10cm) • Delta Ceramcoat White acrylic paint • Tulip Pearl Snow White (or Scribbles Iridescent White Mist) dimensional paint • Delta Ceramcoat matte interior varnish • iridescent crystal glitter • DecoArt Glamour Dust • fabric stiffener • 4"–5" (10cm–13cm) white or ivory round scalloped doily • miniature plastic snowflakes: twelve $^{7}/_{8}$" (2cm) snowflakes and nine $1^{1}/_{4}$" (3cm) snowflakes • glue gun/glue sticks.

1 Basecoat the entire star box with White. Apply trim around the entire edge of the lid using Pearl Snow White dimensional paint. Let dry. Set the lid on the base of the box. Apply trim around the base of the box just under the lid, using the dimensional paint. Repeat for trim around the bottom of the base. Let dry. **2** Apply matte varnish to the base and lid. Immediately sprinkle with iridescent crystal glitter and Glamour Dust while the varnish is still wet. **3** Pour fabric stiffener into a small plastic container or bowl. Dip the doily in the fabric stiffener and remove excess liquid. Place the doily in the center of the lid. Sprinkle the doily with iridescent crystal glitter and Glamour Dust and allow to dry. **4** Hot glue one of the larger plastic snowflakes onto the center of the doily and a smaller snowflake on each point of the star on the lid. Then hot glue the remaining snowflakes randomly along the base of the box. I use snowflakes cut from a snowflake garland, but you can use miniature snowflake ornaments; just remove the hangers.

Teddy Bear Treasures

Who can resist the simple charm of the classic teddy bear, especially during the holiday season? For many of us, this timeless treasure brings back our most cherished memories of Christmases past as we envision its lovable face popping out of Santa's sack of toys.

Our favorite childhood playmate comes to life in a variety of enchanting holiday projects, including a "JOY"-ful stocking swag; a sponged gift bag; a baby's first Christmas keepsake ornament for your precious bundle of joy and a charming Kringle Bear pin, which can also be made into a magnet.

So quick and easy to create, these adorable projects make perfect gifts for the teddy bear collector on your Christmas list. What better way to celebrate the childlike joy of the season than with this huggable, lovable, fuzzy-eared friend!

JOY STOCKING
Garland

*T*his beary delightful swag will spread "JOY" to your holiday home. Fashioned from brown kraft paper, the stockings are accented with miniature jointed bears and attached to a jute "clothesline" with tiny spring clothespins. For a charming variation of the project, attach wire or chenille stem hangers to individually crafted stocking bears for quick-and-easy tree ornaments.

Materials

- paintbrushes and general supplies (see page 6)
- kraft paper (heavy brown paper bags or parcel wrap)
- polyester fiberfill
- Delta Ceramcoat acrylic paint: Cardinal Red, Metallic Kim Gold, Seminole Green, Light Ivory
- Delta Ceramcoat matte interior varnish
- iridescent crystal glitter
- 3½" (9cm), 2" (5cm) and two 1½" (4cm) pieces of 6mm gold tinsel stem
- 5" (13cm) piece of white (gold-accented) glitter stem
- nine ½"–⅝" (1cm–2cm) buttons (four ivory, two red, two green, one gold)
- three 7" (18cm) pieces of ⅛" (3mm) wide gold wired ribbon
- three 2½" (6cm) miniature jointed bears
- two 1" (3cm) miniature pine sprigs (cut from a garland), three miniature artificial red berries, and one miniature 2" (5cm) candy cane
- 24" (61cm) jute twine and six 1" (3cm) spring clothespins
- glue gun/glue sticks

1 CREATE THE STOCKINGS

Referring to the pattern on page 58, trace the stocking shape onto tracing paper. Then slip a piece of transfer paper underneath the traced design and, with a pencil or ballpoint pen, draw the stocking pattern onto a piece of lightweight cardboard or posterboard. Cut out the cardboard template and trace around the stocking template six times onto kraft paper (or a brown paper bag). Cut out the six paper stockings.

Line up the edges of two paper stockings. Hot glue the inside edges together, leaving the top open. Repeat for the other two stockings.

FAMILY STOCKING GARLAND

Instead of having your garland spell JOY, make a stocking with each family member's name. String the stockings together with twine and use the family garland to decorate your mantel or wall.

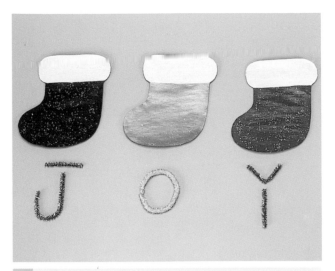

2 PAINT THE STOCKINGS AND FORM THE LETTERS

Basecoat the stockings Cardinal Red, Metallic Kim Gold and Seminole Green, and use Light Ivory for the fur trim. Allow to dry. Apply matte varnish to the stockings, then immediately sprinkle with iridescent crystal glitter while the varnish is still wet.

Next, cut the glitter and tinsel stems for the letters. To make the J, bend the 3½" (9cm) gold tinsel stem into a hook shape and hot glue it onto the red stocking. Hot glue a 1½" (4cm) piece along the top. For the O, bend the 5" (13cm) white glitter stem into a circular shape and hot glue it onto the gold stocking. For the Y, bend the 2" (5cm) gold tinsel stem into a V shape and hot glue it onto the top of the green stocking. Hot glue a 1½" (4cm) piece underneath.

3 HOT GLUE THE BUTTONS AND BOWS

Hot glue buttons onto the fur trim as follows: an ivory, a red and a green button onto the red stocking; an ivory, a gold, then another ivory button onto the gold stocking; and a red, a green and an ivory button onto the green stocking.

Next, cut three 7" (18cm) pieces of gold wired ribbon. Tie each ribbon piece into a bow, trimming the ends to the desired length. Remove the brown bows from around each bear's neck (if necessary) and hot glue the gold bows instead. Stuff each stocking with small pieces of polyester fiberfill.

4 HOT GLUE THE BEARS INTO THE STOCKINGS

Insert the bears into the stockings, posing each one as desired. Hot glue each bear to secure. Hot glue two 1" (3cm) evergreen sprigs (cut from a miniature garland) and three red berries onto the front of the bear in the gold stocking. Hot glue a miniature candy cane beside the bear. Cut a 24" (61cm) piece of jute twine, and tie a small loop at each end of the twine for hanging.

5 ATTACH THE STOCKINGS TO THE TWINE

Using tiny spring clothespins, hang each stocking (spaced evenly) on the twine to spell "JOY."

KRINGLE *Bear Pin*

Dressed as his favorite gift-bearer, this charming Kringle Bear is guaranteed to bring lots of joyful holiday smiles.

Fashioned from air-dry modeling clay, this cute critter can play the role of either a Christmas fridge magnet or decorative pin.

Materials

- paintbrushes and general supplies (see page 6)
- 1¹/₂" (4cm) Styrofoam ball
- air-dry modeling clay (I use Creative Paperclay)
- 1" (3cm) pin clasp
- Delta Ceramcoat acrylic paint: Raw Sienna, Palomino Tan, Charcoal, Light Ivory, Cardinal Red, Spice Brown
- Delta Ceramcoat matte interior spray varnish
- sharp knife
- round wooden toothpick
- glue gun/glue sticks

Tip

To keep your work area clean, lay down wax paper before you begin working with the air-dry modeling clay. The wax paper makes cleanup a snap!

1   **APPLY THE CLAY TO THE STYROFOAM**

Use a sharp knife to cut the Styrofoam ball in half to form the base of the bear's head. You will need only one-half of the Styrofoam ball for each bear pin you make.

   Cover your work surface with wax paper. Apply the air-dry modeling clay onto the surface of the Styrofoam base.

2 FORM THE EAR

For the ear, form a ⁵/₈"–³/₄" (16mm–19mm) ball of clay. Indent the center with your thumb for shape and definition. Press the ear onto the left side of the head until secure. Keep your fingers moist with water and blend the edges until smooth.

3 FORM THE HAT

For the hat, form a 1" (3cm) ball of clay and roll it into a half-moon shape. Press it onto the right side of the head until secure. Blend the edges until smooth.

4 FORM THE MUZZLE

For the muzzle, form three ³/₈"–¹/₂" (10mm–12mm) balls of clay. Press the balls onto the face with two balls side by side and the remaining ball centered underneath. Blend the edges of the muzzle until smooth. Next, use a sharp knife to indent the mouth area.

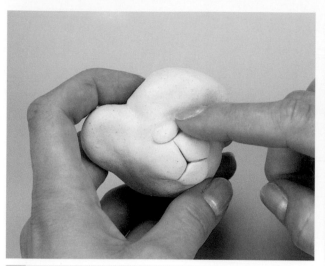

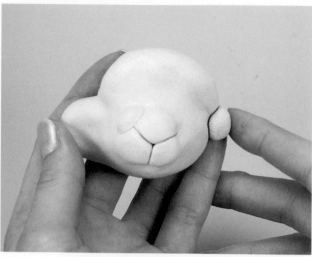

5 FORM THE NOSE

For the nose, form a ¼" (6mm) ball of clay and press it onto the top center of the muzzle. Blend the edges until smooth.

6 ADD THE POM-POM

For the pom-pom, form a ⅜" (10mm) ball of clay and press it onto the bottom of the hat. Blend the edges until smooth. Use a wooden toothpick to place indentations for texture, then allow to dry.

7 PAINT THE BEAR AND ADD A PIN CLASP

First, basecoat the bear with Raw Sienna and let dry. To paint the facial features, refer to the pattern on page 58. Paint the muzzle and inside of the ear with Palomino Tan. Use Charcoal for the eyes, nose, mouth, freckles and eyebrows. Paint the pupils and create a highlight on the nose using Light Ivory. For the cheeks, drybrush with Cardinal Red and create cheek highlights using Light Ivory. Allow to dry.

Next, paint the hat with Cardinal Red and let dry. Then, paint dots on the hat using Light Ivory. Also use Light Ivory for the pom-pom. Let dry.

To complete the bear, antique it with a wash of Spice Brown and allow to dry. Then apply matte varnish. When dry, hot glue a 1" (3cm) pin clasp onto the back of the bear head.

MAKE IT A MAGNET!

The Kringle Bear makes a great refrigerator magnet, too! Simply hot glue a ¾" (2cm) magnet to the back of the bear instead of the pin.

BABY'S FIRST CHRISTMAS ORNAMENT

MATERIALS: PAINTBRUSHES AND GENERAL SUPPLIES (SEE PAGE 6) • 2⅝" (7cm) glass ball ornament • Delta Ceramcoat acrylic paint: Lisa Pink, Blue Heaven (boy ornament only), Raw Sienna, Palomino Tan, Charcoal, Light Ivory • Delta Ceramcoat matte interior spray varnish • small pieces of sponge • fine-point black permanent pen • old, worn toothbrush. **OPTIONAL:** wooden dowel and floral foam brick (for drying) • personalized tag • pink, white and blue curling ribbon • pink or blue ⅛" (3mm) satin bow • decorative edge scissors • hole punch.

1 Remove the top ornament hanger. Using a small piece of dampened sponge, apply Lisa Pink (girl ornament) or Blue Heaven (boy ornament) onto the surface of the glass ball. (**OPTIONAL:** Insert a wooden dowel into the open hole of the ornament and a floral foam brick for easier drying.) Apply two or three coats for solid coverage. **2** To paint the bears, refer to the pattern on page 58. Basecoat the bear head Raw Sienna. Paint the muzzle Palomino Tan. Use Charcoal for the eyes and Light Ivory for the pupils. Paint the nose Charcoal with a Light Ivory highlight dot. Use Charcoal for the mouth and freckles. For the cheeks and inside of the ears, drybrush with Lisa Pink and use Light Ivory for highlight dots. **3** Use a black permanent pen to outline the bear head and to write a name and date. Apply Light Ivory dots around the surface of the ornament. Allow to dry. Use a toothbrush to spatter with Light Ivory. Apply matte varnish. Reinsert the top ornament hanger. **4** **OPTIONAL:** Add a personalized tag, using cardstock cut with decorative edge scissors. Accent the ornament with pink, white and blue curling ribbon and a pink or blue bow.

THREE BEARS GIFT BAG

MATERIALS: PAINTBRUSHES AND GENERAL SUPPLIES (SEE PAGE 6) • 10½" x 8" (27cm x 20cm) white kraft tote bag • Delta Ceramcoat acrylic paint: Raw Sienna, Palomino Tan, Charcoal, Light Ivory, Cardinal Red • Delta Ceramcoat matte interior spray varnish • four ½" (1cm) buttons: three red, one green • six green cedar sprigs • nine artificial red berries • five snowflake buttons or miniature ornaments • three strands red raffia • 1" x 5" (3cm x 13cm) red/green plaid fabric strip • Miracle Sponge compressed sponge sheets • old, worn toothbrush • fine-point black permanent pen • glue gun/glue sticks.

1 Transfer the head, ear and muzzle shapes (see page 59) onto a sheet of compressed sponge and cut them out (see Sponge Painting on page 8 for more information). Dampen the sponges with water (damp, not wet), and then sponge paint the head and ears with Raw Sienna and let dry. Sponge paint the muzzle with Palomino Tan. Repeat for the remaining two bears, using the photo at the right for placement. Let dry. **2** Next, paint the eyes Charcoal with Light Ivory pupils. Drybrush the cheeks and inside each ear with Cardinal Red. Add cheek highlights using Light Ivory. **3** Use a fine-point black pen to outline the bear shapes and add the eyebrows, mouth and freckles (see the pattern on page 59). Next, spatter the bag with Light Ivory, then lightly mist with matte spray varnish. **4** Hot glue the red button noses, sprigs, berries and snowflakes onto the bag. Add a raffia bow, knotted fabric bow, and a green button to the handle.

Glitters of Christmas Past

Add a glittering touch of elegance to your Christmas décor with these fanciful decorations crafted in the rich tradition of the Victorian era. Fashioned from shimmering gold accents, paper scraps and ornate trims, these exquisite projects will take you back to a bygone Christmas exuding opulence and romantic charm.

Old-world Santa images adorn a gilded paper stocking and a keepsake book—perfect for a nostalgic holiday celebration. From the heavens, an angelic Santa appears to decorate your home with starry-eyed wonder. And if you enjoy cozy fires during the holiday season, adorn your hearth with the Victorian Heart Box to hold your matches. These "glitters of Christmas past" are sure to become old-fashioned holiday favorites.

VICTORIAN SANTA
Stocking

This kraft paper stocking decorated with an old-world Santa image and Victorian-style trims is so elegant—yet so simple to make! Hang this exquisite creation early in the season so you can enjoy its vintage charm all through the holidays.

Materials

- general supplies (see page 6)
- kraft paper (such as heavy brown paper bags or parcel wrap)
- polyester fiberfill
- Delta Ceramcoat acrylic paint: Light Ivory, Metallic Kim Gold
- Tulip Pearl Gold (or Scribbles Iridescent Gold) dimensional paint
- Delta Ceramcoat matte interior spray varnish
- iridescent crystal glitter
- 5" (13cm) round gold or white paper doily
- 7" x 4½" (18cm x 11cm) Victorian Santa image from scrapbook paper, gift wrap or a greeting card
- three ½" (1cm) gold star stickers, two 1½"–1¾" (4cm–5cm) artificial green leaves, and three miniature artificial red berries
- 15" (38cm) of ½" (1cm) wide gold wired ribbon
- ⅝" (2cm) gold jingle bell
- 12" (30cm) 6mm gold tinsel stem
- small piece of sponge
- tacky glue
- glue gun/glue sticks

1 CUT OUT THE STOCKING

Referring to the stocking pattern on page 57, use a pencil to trace the stocking shape onto tracing paper. Slip a piece of transfer paper underneath the tracing paper and, with a pencil or ballpoint pen, draw the stocking pattern twice onto kraft paper (or a brown paper bag). Then cut out the two paper stockings and line up the edges. Hot glue the inside edges together, leaving the top completely open to stuff fiberfill after the stocking is painted and decorated.

Tip

If you plan to make several stockings, transfer the pattern onto a piece of lightweight cardboard or posterboard to make a permanent stocking template. You can use this template to make several Victorian Stockings. If you made a template for the Old-World Santa Stocking on page 24, you don't need to make another. The stocking is the same size for both projects. See page 54 for more information on transferring patterns and creating templates.

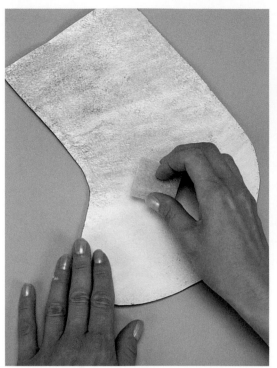

3 APPLY DIMENSIONAL PAINT FOR THE TRIM

Use Pearl Gold dimensional paint to apply trim along the outer edge of the stocking, then let dry.

Next, cut a 5" (13cm) gold paper doily in half. (If you are using a white doily, sponge paint it with Metallic Kim Gold and let dry.) Use tacky glue to attach the doily onto the top center of the stocking. Press the edges to flatten.

2 PAINT THE STOCKING

Use a piece of dampened sponge to apply Light Ivory to the paper stocking. Apply two or three coats as necessary until solid coverage is obtained. Let dry.

Next, using the damp sponge, very sparingly apply Metallic Kim Gold paint to give a subtle textured effect. Let dry.

4 CUT OUT THE SANTA IMAGE

Cut the Santa image from scrapbook paper, gift wrap or a greeting card. Use tacky glue to attach the Santa image to the center of the stocking. Press the edges to flatten and let dry.

Next, apply three gold star stickers. Apply matte spray varnish to the entire stocking (including the doily and the Santa image), then immediately sprinkle with iridescent crystal glitter while the varnish is still wet. Apply matte varnish to two green leaves and three red berries and sprinkle with glitter. Hot glue the leaves and berries onto the top of the stocking.

To finish the embellishing, cut 15" (38cm) of gold wired ribbon. Tie a bow, then trim the ends to the desired length. Hot glue the bow onto the top of the stocking just under the leaves and berries. Hot glue the gold jingle bell onto the toe of the stocking. Next, stuff polyester fiberfill inside the stocking. Then, hot glue a 12" (30cm) gold tinsel stem inside the stocking for the hanger. Fill the stocking with your favorite treats.

HEAVENLY SANTA
Decoration

A heavenly holiday treasure, this angelic Santa is exquisitely crafted yet surprisingly simple to make. The face is sculpted from air-dry modeling clay and adorned with a natural wool beard. His gilded cardboard body is embellished with gold trim and charming star buttons. In keeping with the heavenly theme, a gold tinsel halo and shimmering ribbon "wings" provide an elegant finishing touch.

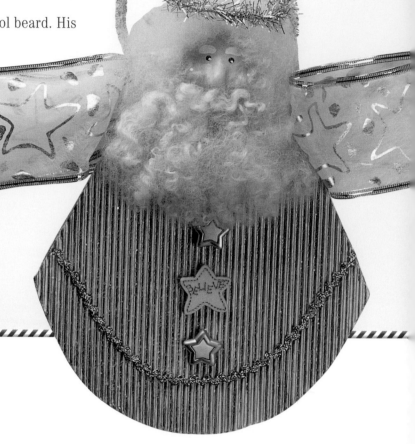

Materials

- paintbrushes and general supplies (see page 6)
- air-dry modeling clay (I use Creative Paperclay)
- two 8¹/₂" x 11" (22cm x 28cm) pieces of corrugated cardboard
- Delta Ceramcoat acrylic paint: Light Ivory, Metallic Kim Gold, Fleshtone, Charcoal, Cardinal Red, Spice Brown,
- Delta Ceramcoat matte interior varnish
- iridescent crystal glitter
- natural wool doll hair (see Resources page 61)
- 6" (15cm) piece of 15mm gold tinsel stem
- 25" (64cm) of 2¹/₂" (6cm) wide gold (or gold-accented) wired ribbon
- small piece of gold wire
- 12" (30cm) piece of 6mm white (gold-accented) glitter stem
- 8³/₄" (22cm) gold rickrack trim
- three ¾"–1" (2cm–3cm) star buttons (see Specialty Resources page 62)
- small piece of sponge
- glue gun/glue sticks

Tip

To save time, make a permanent Santa body template. So the next time you want to make the Heavenly Santa, you are ready to trace the template directly onto the cardboard. See Using Patterns & Templates on page 54 for more information.

1 FORM THE BASE

Cover your work surface with wax paper. Form a 1½" (4cm) ball of air-dry modeling clay, and following the pattern on page 60, flatten slightly to form the Santa face.

2 FORM THE NOSE

Form a ⅜"–½" (10mm–13mm) ball of clay. Roll it into a nose shape, then press it onto the center of the face. Dip your fingers in a bowl of warm water to moisten, then blend the edges of the nose until smooth.

3 FORM THE CHEEKS

Form two balls of clay, approximately ⅜"–½" (10mm–13mm) each. Press the two balls onto each side of the nose for cheeks. Blend the edges until smooth. Allow the clay face to dry.

4 CREATE THE BODY

Referring to the pattern on page 60, trace the body shape onto tracing paper. Slip a piece of transfer paper underneath the tracing paper and, with a pencil or ballpoint pen, draw the body pattern twice, once onto each backside (smooth side) piece of corrugated cardboard. (I traced the design so the cardboard ridges run vertically.) Cut out the two cardboard body pieces and hot glue the backside two pieces together. Use scissors to trim any overlapping edges.

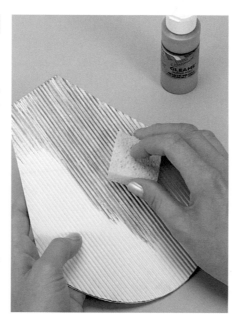

Next, basecoat both sides of the cardboard body with Light Ivory and let dry. Using a dampened piece of sponge, apply Metallic Kim Gold for a shimmering effect, moving down the creases for a light application. Allow to dry. Apply matte varnish to the cardboard body, then immediately sprinkle with iridescent crystal glitter while the varnish is still wet.

5 PAINT THE SANTA FACE

Once the clay has dried, basecoat the Santa face with Fleshtone and let dry. Paint the eyes using Charcoal and add Light Ivory for the pupils. Use Light Ivory for the eyebrows, and drybrush the cheeks with Cardinal Red. Add Light Ivory cheek highlights to complete the features.

To antique the face, apply a wash of Spice Brown. When dry, apply matte varnish.

6 HOT GLUE THE WOOL HAIR →

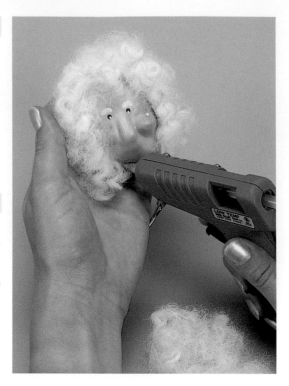

Hot glue the wool doll hair onto the head and face for Santa's hair, beard and mustache. Use your fingers to fluff it into the desired shape. (I use Curly Crepe craft hair in white, but Wavy Wool in natural is another brand that works well. See the Resources section on page 61.)

For the halo, cut a 6" (15cm) piece of gold tinsel stem. Hot glue the stem into a circular shape, then glue it onto Santa's head. Next, hot glue the head onto the top of the cardboard body.

7 ADD THE WINGS, HANGER AND TRIMS

For the wings, cut a 25" (64cm) piece of 2½" (6cm) wide gold wired ribbon. Fold each end over to meet in the center, then hot glue the ends to secure. Tie the center of the wings with a small piece of gold wire. Hot glue the wings to the back of the Santa body. Next, hot glue a 12" (30cm) white glitter stem onto the back of the Santa for a hanger.

Cut an 8¾" (22cm) piece of gold rickrack trim. Hot glue the trim along the bottom edge of the body, approximately 1" (3cm) from the bottom. For the finishing touch, hot glue three star buttons down the front center of the body.

MAKE A TREE TOPPER

Let this Victorian Santa be your Christmas tree angel. Instead of attaching a glitter stem hanger, use wire to attach the Heavenly Santa to the top of your tree.

CHRISTMAS MEMORY BOOK

MATERIALS: GENERAL SUPPLIES (SEE PAGE 6) • 6" x 8" (15cm x 20cm) ivory memory book • Delta Ceramcoat Metallic Kim Gold acrylic paint • Delta Ceramcoat matte interior spray varnish • iridescent crystal glitter • 5" x 7" (13cm x 18cm) piece ivory cardstock • Victorian Santa postcard, trimmed to 3½" x 5½" (9cm x 14cm) • 12" (30cm) 6mm gold tinsel stems: two 7" (18cm) pieces and two 5" (13cm) pieces • four ½" (1cm) gold buttons • three 1¼" (3cm) pine sprigs, cut from a miniature garland • three miniature artificial red berries • 12" (30cm) of ⅛" (3mm) wide gold wired ribbon • small piece of sponge • tacky glue • glue gun/glue sticks.

1 Cut out a 5" x 7" (13cm x 18cm) piece of ivory cardstock. Using a damp piece of sponge, apply Metallic Kim Gold onto the piece of cardstock. Let dry. Use tacky glue to attach the gold-painted cardstock onto the center of the memory book. Let dry. **2** Trim a Santa postcard or greeting card to 3½" x 5½" (9cm x 14cm) and glue it onto the center of the painted cardstock. Let dry. Apply matte varnish then immediately sprinkle with iridescent crystal glitter while varnish is still wet. **3** Cut two 7" (18cm) and two 5" (13cm) pieces of gold tinsel stems and hot glue them around the painted cardstock. Then hot glue a gold button onto each corner. **4** Cut three pine sprigs approximately 1¼" (3cm) long. Apply matte varnish to the pine sprigs and berries, then immediately sprinkle with iridescent crystal glitter while the varnish is still wet. Hot glue the pine sprigs then three berries onto the top of the keepsake book. **5** Cut a 12" (30cm) piece of ⅛" (3mm) wide gold wired ribbon and tie a bow. Trim the ends to the desired length, and hot glue the bow onto the bottom of the book.

VICTORIAN HEART BOX

MATERIALS: GENERAL SUPPLIES (SEE PAGE 6) • 12" x 3¼" (30cm x 8cm) papier mâché box • Delta Ceramcoat acrylic paint: Light Ivory, Metallic Kim Gold • Tulip Pearl Antique Gold (or Scribbles Glittering Gold) dimensional paint • Delta Ceramcoat matte interior varnish • iridescent crystal glitter • gold glitter • 4½" (11cm) Rusty Tin-Tiques Folk Heart • 14" (36cm) piece of ½" (1cm) wide gold wired ribbon • ½" (1cm) ivory button • three 1¼" (3cm) pine sprigs, cut from a miniature garland • three miniature artificial red berries • two 14" (36cm) pieces of ⅜" (10mm) wide gold scalloped trim • small pieces of sponge • glue gun/glue sticks.

1 Apply two to three coats of Light Ivory to the box with a damp sponge. Next, lightly sponge Metallic Kim Gold for texture, and apply more gold paint on the edges. Apply matte varnish, immediately sprinkling with crystal and gold glitters. **2** Sponge Metallic Kim Gold onto the heart. Use dimensional paint for the trim and dots around the edge of the heart. When dry, apply matte varnish, immediately sprinkling with iridescent crystal glitter. Hot glue the heart onto the box's center. **3** Make a bow from the piece of gold wired ribbon and hot glue it onto the top of the heart. Hot glue an ivory button onto the bow's center. Apply matte varnish to the pine sprigs and berries, immediately sprinkling with iridescent crystal glitter. Hot glue the pine sprigs, then the three berries onto the top of the tin heart. To finish, hot glue a piece of gold trim along the top and bottom of the box.

using patterns & templates

★ TRANSFERRING PATTERNS

Use a pencil to trace the desired pattern onto a sheet of transparent tracing paper. Insert a piece of gray transfer paper in between the traced pattern and your surface area. Using a pencil or ballpoint pen, retrace the pattern, transferring it to your surface. Since the transfer paper is coated on only one side, be sure the correct side is facing down by making a small mark to test.

★ PAINTING DETAILS

Most of the projects in this book are painted in a very simple style. So if you prefer, instead of transferring the basecoated areas and finer details, you can sketch them freehand with a pencil, using the pattern or finished project as a visual reference. Remember to basecoat all areas first before sketching or transferring the finer details.

★ CREATING TEMPLATES

When making any of the kraft paper projects, such as the Gingerbread Boy Decoration (page 16), I find it easier to create a permanent template first.

Instead of transferring each shape directly onto the kraft paper, transfer the shape onto a piece of lightweight cardboard or posterboard to make a cardboard template. You can use this template over and over again by simply tracing around the outer edges with a pencil. This technique will save you oodles of time, especially if you plan to make several projects requiring the same basic shape.

You can also use this technique to transfer shapes onto compressed sponges and corrugated cardboard (like for the Three Bears Gift Bag on page 45 and the Heavenly Santa on page 50).

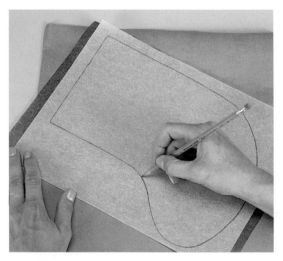

Using Tracing Paper to Transfer a Pattern

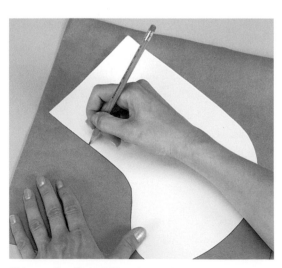

Using a Cardboard Template to Trace a Pattern

[SPECIAL NOTE]

CHEEK PATTERNS

Do not transfer the cheek areas. They were drawn on the patterns simply for visual reference only. Since the cheeks are softly dry-brushed, it will be difficult to cover the line left if the cheek area is transferred or sketched.

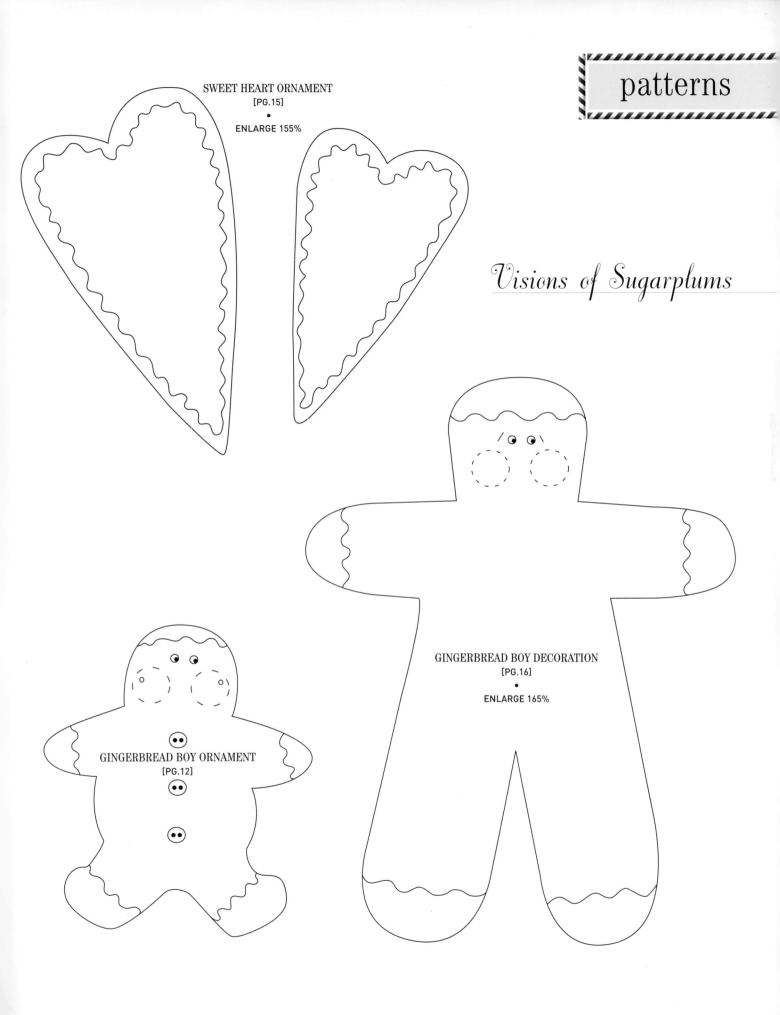

SWEET HEART ORNAMENT
[PG.15]
•
ENLARGE 155%

Visions of Sugarplums

GINGERBREAD BOY DECORATION
[PG.16]
•
ENLARGE 165%

GINGERBREAD BOY ORNAMENT
[PG.12]

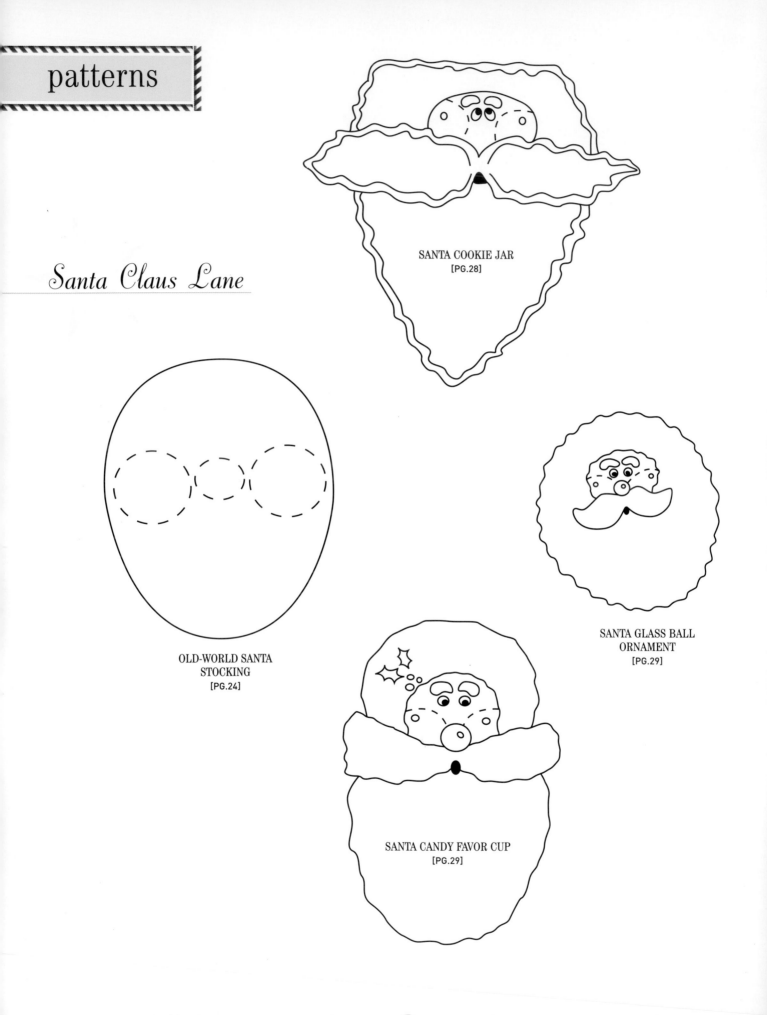

patterns

Santa Claus Lane

SANTA COOKIE JAR
[PG.28]

OLD-WORLD SANTA
STOCKING
[PG.24]

SANTA GLASS BALL
ORNAMENT
[PG.29]

SANTA CANDY FAVOR CUP
[PG.29]

OLD-WORLD SANTA STOCKING
[PG.24]

&

VICTORIAN SANTA STOCKING
[PG.48]

•

ENLARGE 120%

patterns

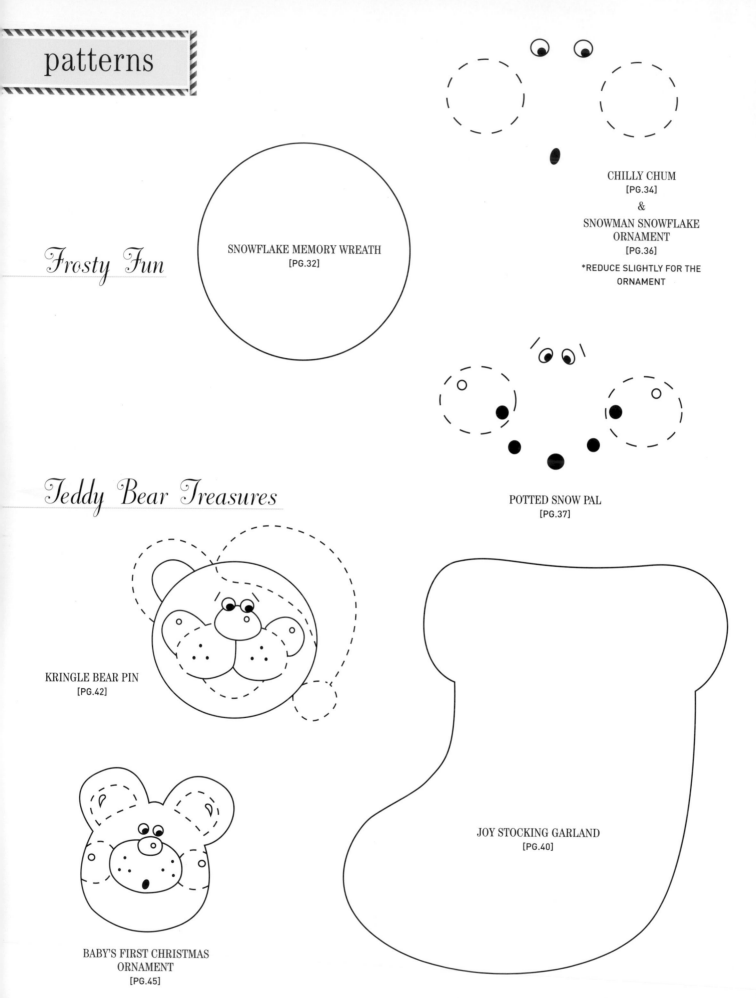

Frosty Fun

SNOWFLAKE MEMORY WREATH
[PG.32]

CHILLY CHUM
[PG.34]
&
SNOWMAN SNOWFLAKE
ORNAMENT
[PG.36]
*REDUCE SLIGHTLY FOR THE
ORNAMENT

POTTED SNOW PAL
[PG.37]

Teddy Bear Treasures

KRINGLE BEAR PIN
[PG.42]

JOY STOCKING GARLAND
[PG.40]

BABY'S FIRST CHRISTMAS
ORNAMENT
[PG.45]

THREE BEARS GIFT BAG
[PG.45]

•

ENLARGE 125%

HEAD
•
ACTUAL SIZE

EAR
•
ACTUAL SIZE

MUZZLE
•
ACTUAL SIZE

Glitters of Christmas Past

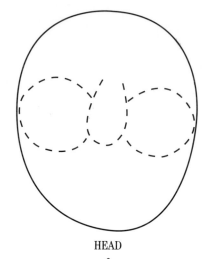

HEAD

•

ACTUAL SIZE

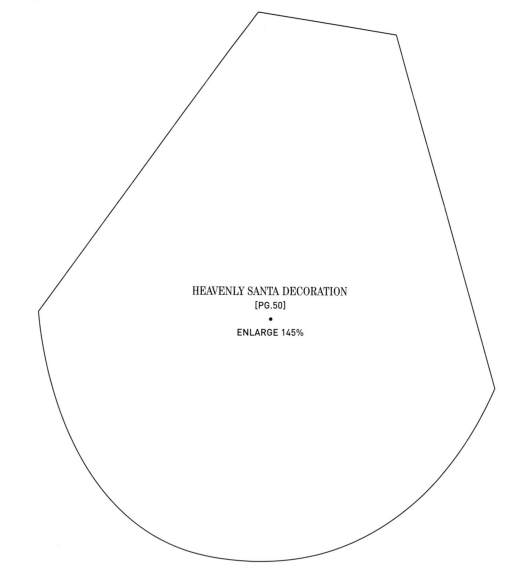

HEAVENLY SANTA DECORATION
[PG.50]

•

ENLARGE 145%

GENERAL MATERIALS

Activa Products, Inc.
P.O. Box 1296
Marshall, TX 75671
www.activa-products.com

• *Celluclay Instant Papier Mâché*

All Cooped Up Designs
560 S. State #B1
Orem, Utah 84058
(800) 498-1517 or (801) 226-1517
www.allcoopedup.com

• *Curly Crepe craft hair*

The Color Wheel Company
P.O. Box 130
Philomath, OR 97370-0130
(541) 929-7526
www.colorwheelco.com

• *Miracle Sponge (compressed sponges that expand when wet)*

Creative Paperclay Company, Inc.
79 Daily Drive, Suite 101
Camarillo, CA 93010
(800) 899-5952 or (805) 484-6648
www.paperclay.com

• *Creative Paperclay modeling compound*

DecoArt, Inc.
P.O. Box 386
Stanford, KY 40484
(800) 477-8478 or (606) 365-3193
www.decoart.com

• *Snow-Tex and Glamour Dust; also a great source for acrylic craft paints and general painting supplies*

Delta Technical Coatings, Inc.
2550 Pellissier Place
Whittier, CA 90601
(800) 423-4135 or (562) 695-7969
www.deltacrafts.com

• *Delta Ceramcoat acrylic paints, matte interior and spray varnishes, gesso, Freshly Fallen Snow and general painting supplies*

Duncan Enterprises, Inc.
5673 E. Shields Avenue
Fresno, CA 93727
(800) 438-6226 or (559) 291-4444
E-MAIL: consumer@duncanmail.com
www.duncancrafts.com

• *Tulip and Scribbles dimensional paints*

FloraCraft (Dow Styrofoam)
One Longfellow Place
P.O. Box 400
Ludington, MI 49431
(800) 253-0409 or (231) 845-5127
E-MAIL: postmaster@floracraft.com
www.floracraft.com
www.styrofoamcrafts.com

• *Styrofoam brand plastic foam products*

Loew-Cornell, Inc.
563 Chestnut Avenue
Teaneck, NJ 07666-2490
(201) 836-7070
E-MAIL: loew-cornell@loew-cornell.com
www.loew-cornell.com

• *paintbrushes, palette knives and general painting supplies*

One & Only Creations
P.O. Box 2730
68 Coombs Street, Suite N
Napa, CA 94559
(800) 262-6768 or (707) 255-8033
www.oneandonlycreations.com

• *Wavy Wool natural wool doll hair*

specialty resources

CRAFT TRIMS & SPECIALTY PRODUCTS

The following list contains contact information for some of the specialty items used to craft the projects. For a general resource list, please see page 61.

★ ARTIFICIAL CANDIES

PROJECT: Sugarplum Cottage, page 14
[candies cut from 9' (3m) candy garland]

AVAILABLE FROM:
Kurt S. Adler, Inc.
New York, NY 10010
www.kurtadler.com

★ CLEAR ACRYLIC SNOWFLAKE ORNAMENT
[6½" (17CM)]

PROJECT: Snowman Snowflake Ornament, page 36

DISTRIBUTED BY:
Sterling, Inc.
Kansas City, MO 64108

AVAILABLE FROM: Christmas Corner, Menards, Seasonal Concepts and specialty Christmas stores across the country.

> • *There are several manufacturers of acrylic snowflakes. Different brands are available from specialty Christmas stores and general housewares stores, such as Menards and Canadian Tire.*

★ MEMORY BOOK

PROJECT: Christmas Memory Book, page 53

AVAILABLE FROM:
Paper Reflections
DMD Industries, Inc.
2300 S. Old Missouri Road
Springdale, AR 72764
www.dmdind.com

★ MINIATURE DECORATIVE SKIS

PROJECT: Chilly Chum, page 34

AVAILABLE FROM: most major arts and crafts or hobby stores

> • *Skis and poles may be sold unpainted. Paint and embellish as desired.*

★ MINIATURE SNOWSHOES

PROJECT: North Woods Santa, page 20

AVAILABLE FROM:
Mangelsen's
Westgate Plaza
3457 South 84th Street
Omaha, NE 68124
(402) 391-6225
www.mangelsens.com

★ OLD-FASHIONED SANTA CLAUS POSTCARDS

PROJECT: Christmas Memory Book, page 53

AVAILABLE FROM:
Dover Publications
31 East 2nd Street
Mineola, NY 11501-3852
www.doverpublications.com

★ STAR BUTTONS

PROJECT: Heavenly Santa Decoration, page 50

AVAILABLE FROM: all major arts and crafts stores

> • *Dress It Up collection is a registered trademark of Jesse James & Co. Inc. www.JesseJamesButton.com*

index

CELEBRATE YOUR FAVORITE HOLIDAYS WITH CRAFTS FROM NORTH LIGHT BOOKS!

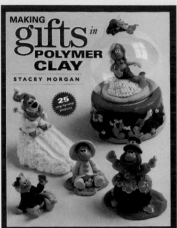

SILK FLORALS FOR THE HOLIDAYS • Make your holidays brighter and more special by creating your very own floral décor! Cele Kahle shows you how to create a variety of gorgeous arrangements, swags, topiaries, wreaths and more. You'll create 19 projects in all, using silk foliage, berries, fruit and ribbon. Each one comes with step-by-step guidelines and beautiful full-color photos.

ISBN 1-58180-259-5, paperback, 128 pages, #32124-K

EASY CHRISTMAS PROJECTS YOU CAN PAINT • Create classic holiday decorations that everyone will love! You'll find 14 simple painting projects inside, from Santa figures and Christmas card holders to tree ornaments and candy dishes. Each one includes easy-to-follow instructions, step-by-step photographs and simple designs that you can use on candles, fabric or glass.

ISBN 1-58180-237-4, paperback, 112 pages, #32012-K

WREATHS FOR EVERY SEASON • These 20 beautiful wreath projects are perfect for celebrating those special times of year. You'll find a range of sizes and styles, utilizing a variety of creative materials, including dried herbs, cinnamon sticks, silk flowers, autumn leaves, Christmas candy and more. Clear, step-by-step instructions ensure beautiful, long-lasting results every time!

ISBN 1-58180-239-0, paperback, 144 pages, #32015-K

MAKING GIFTS IN POLYMER CLAY • These 21 adorable projects perfectly capture the spirit of the seasons. Each one is easy to make and simple enough to be completed in a single sitting. From leprechauns, Easter eggs and spooky witches to Thanksgiving turkeys and a polar bear on skis, there's something for everyone—including kids! You'll also find guidelines for creating magnets, buttons and pins.

ISBN 1-58180-104-1, paperback, 128 pages, #31792-K

These books and other fine North Light titles are available from your local arts & crafts retailer, bookstore, online supplier or by calling 1-800-448-0915